Recollections and Reflections

Douglas Black

DOUGLAS BLACK

Recollections and Reflections

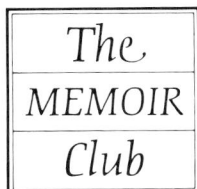

The
MEMOIR
Club

ISBN 0 7279 0209 1

Made and printed in Great Britain by
Cambridge University Press

To Mollie

Contents

Foreword

The story of our lives can be described quite simply. We are born: we grow up: if we are fortunate, we marry someone with whom we can spend the rest of our lives: and in the fullness of time, we die. More picturesquely and poignantly, we are like the sparrow, described to Edwin of Northumbria, which flies into a lighted banqueting hall, and then flies out again into the darkness; or like Edmund Waller's lovely rose, in which could be read

> How small a part of time they share,
> That are so wondrous sweet and fair.

But these elegiac simplicities do not make a book; and in any case this is not an autobiography. So perhaps you will forgive me the occasional complexity, in the spirit of the German motto, "Warum einfach machen, wenn man kann es komplizieren?"*

The plan of this book is that the first chapter, which gives an annotated chronological framework, is followed by a number of chapters bearing memories and reflections on themes that have bulked large in my professional life. Although the treatment of these themes is inescapably personal, the main focus is not on my private life. But I would be churlish indeed if I were not to say that whatever there has been of grace and pleasure in my life, I owe it in the early years to a happy home and loving parents; and later to my wife above all, to my children, and also to the many friends with whom I have been privileged to work.

* Why do something simply when you can complicate it?

I doubt if this book would have been written had it not been for a suggestion from Stephen Lock that I should "write my memoirs." Even when it became apparent that something less formal was all I could do, he gave me the most practical assistance by providing not only a tape recorder but also a secretary who could both read my writing and understand my accent, Evelyn Aldie Gallagher. I am most grateful to them both.

1 A framework

It may seem an odd way to begin a collection of reminiscences, but let me confess that all my life I have been plagued by occasional — and disconcertingly random — instances of minor departure from accuracy. I do not mean that I am habitually or deliberately deceptive or inaccurate, merely that what I recapture from any event is the gist of the happening and not a picture of photographic accuracy. The good side of this is that it breeds a necessary addiction to works of reference on any serious occasion: the bad side is that I may occasionally mislead without intending to; and in this imperfect world innocence of intention does not always protect against a dire outcome. "I didn't mean to" is a defence which may help a child, but scarcely an adult. So if poetry takes its origin from emotion recollected in tranquillity, perhaps my own recollections are essentially true to fact, but blurred at the margin by retrospective uncertainty.

For example, I can remember the impact of reading a translation of Herodotus in my early teens, and even the grey-blue binding of the book, which came long before the Penguin Classics translation by Aubrey de Selincourt, which I have since read, or dipped into, many times. But I cannot remember in what year I read it, or how old I was exactly, or what made me choose it. On the other hand, I do recall the remark of Solon the Athenian to Croesus of Lydia, echoed by Croesus himself when on a funeral pyre — courtesy of Cyrus — and happily resulting in Croesus's survival: "Call no man happy till he dies, he is at best but fortunate."*

* Herodotus. *Histories*, i; 32

This saying may serve both as a text — or leitmotiv — for this book, because anyone who has survived two world wars and various other hazards of this century may count himself fortunate; and also as a solid reason for not attempting anything so formal and pretentious as an autobiography. In general, I propose to arrange my memories by theme rather than by timing; but in this introductory chapter it may be appropriate to set out a chronological framework, which may serve two distinct ends. The way in which I set it out, and the types of experience that I enjoyed at different times, may tell the reader what sort of man I am; and he will also be able to judge in general terms my degree of maturity at the time of any events that I may describe, and so tincture my opinion of them with the appropriate gloss for my immaturity in some cases, or postmaturity in others.

I was born on 29 May 1913, the anniversary of Charles II's entry into London in 1660, and of the capture of Constantinople by Mohammed the Ottoman in 1453. The first of these antecedent events is generally looked on as auspicious, the second less so; thus I started life on a neutral day, in the parish of Delting, Shetland, where my father was minister at the time. If I may relieve the reader of a natural misapprehension, this announcement of my birth does not usher in a long recital of childhood memories, such as are largely based on misery and deprivation. I remember nothing of Delting, having left it at the age of 2, and it is now just a puzzling entry on my passport. Most of my boyhood was spent in Kirriemuir, the "Thrums" of J M Barrie. My father's stipend peaked at £300 a year, but we had plenty of good food, fresh air, and books. My mother, who had been a ward sister in Dundee Royal Infirmary, had kept a book on elementary physiology by Sir Michael Foster, which awakened my interest in how our bodies work.

The school in Kirriemuir was Webster's Seminary, which in spite of its name was as far removed from popery as could be; the English master was Mr Moore, darkly rumoured to be a socialist and to have been a "conchie" in the war, but luckily for me an enthusiast for his subject. When I was 14 we moved to a country parish, Inverarity, between Forfar and Dundee; I moved also to Forfar Academy, where Mr Allardyce gave me an abiding love for Latin language and literature. The subjects that I took in the Scottish Higher Certificate of Education (intermediate in standard between O and A levels in the English GCE) were English, Latin, and physics and chemistry; so in a fashion I had spanned the two cultures, at a lowly level, before C P Snow invented them.

My medical course at St Andrews University lasted six years, from 1929 to 1936, and was equally divided between the preclinical school at St Andrews, and the clinical years at the Royal Infirmary in Dundee. In those days there was no difficulty about entering medical school, if you could pass the Higher School Certificate and find the money. On entry I was advised to take the optional degree of Bachelor of Science, in addition to the obligatory degrees of Bachelor of Medicine and Surgery. With little comprehension of the issues, but elated perhaps by the award of a bursary, I agreed; it turned out that the course consisted largely of repeating the second year lecture course in physiology in the third year, and learning some embryology, which I have since forgotten. The immediate benefit was the opportunity of spending an additional year in St Andrews; another unexpected benefit came later, which well illustrates the part played by luck in human affairs, but of that in its proper place.

The medical course then was less intensive than it is now, with instruction largely given in the Scotch style by formal lectures, and with long holidays at Christmas, Easter, and in the summer. Then as now, there were differing views on the value of the medical course — some doctors come out of it convinced that they have learnt everything that matters; some lay observers reckon that it teaches nothing worth while. The truth no doubt lies somewhere in between, as it so often does. The lectures and the stimulus of annual examinations made us learn the facts, as they were then understood — some of them have since changed; but what really moulded us into doctors was to some extent our teachers and fellow students, and to a rather greater extent the hours that we spent with patients in casualty, in clinics, and on the wards. My great friend of student days, Jim White, who later became a surgeon in Penzance, shared digs with me hard by the hospital, and we did a whole series of unofficial clerkships in addition to the set pieces.

After qualifying, I did a resident post with Adam Patrick, the professor of medicine, a man of few but weighty words, who would come up at night to do blood sugars in the ward side room — clinical pathologists and biochemists had not yet been invented. My second resident post was with Francis Brown, a superb operating surgeon who could never be tempted into the wards; and with his junior, Walter Campbell, who did the acute abdomens, and would deliver a Parthian instruction to leave a pint of saline in the peritoneal cavity. An instinct that there might be more to it than that aroused an interest in electrolytes and body fluid that was to stay with me for many a year.

In those days, with comparatively little specialist medical treatment available, there was less of a distinction between physicians and general practitioners; and medical emergencies about which anything could effectively be done were fewer than the unavoidable acute surgery. So it was possible to be on call medically on alternate days, and even to give the emergency anaesthetics when on medical call — an arrangement that probably contributed more to the experience of the doctor than to the welfare of the patient. Between the two six month periods of residence there was a holiday of one weekend; and study leave was something else that had not been invented. We learnt by the principles practised by Wackford Squeers, a somewhat underrated pedagogue, but not a good example: first spell "winder," and then clean it.

Among the common medical emergencies was haematemesis, the vomiting of blood from the upper alimentary tract. The desperate regimen of giving those unfortunate patients nothing to eat, just ice to suck, was being questioned by Meulengracht in Copenhagen and Leslie Witts at Barts.

4

I became interested in the problem and without too much hope put in for a Medical Research Council studentship for clinical research, in the very first year in which they were offered — another piece of luck? It was part of the design that those appointed should go to a medical school other than their own; and I was delighted not simply to get the studentship (after all, it was worth £200 a year), but also to be asked to work under the supervision of Leslie Witts, who was moving to the newly opened Nuffield department of clinical medicine at Oxford. This was wealth, in the purely academic sense, beyond the dreams of avarice.

Months later, after I had been in Oxford for some time, I discovered by implication one possible reason for my good fortune, in the form of a delayed benefit from my intercalated BSc at St Andrews. One day my chief asked me what had been the topic of my research for the BSc. (I have explained a little earlier the modest nature of my own BSc, very different from the research based Oxford BSc.) My puzzlement came immediately, followed by slight embarrassment; Leslie Witts's no doubt came later, but we lived it down, and this puppy is very grateful to him for the shape into which he licked me, with some knowledge of how to do research and to write a scientific paper.

My few years in Oxford were very happy ones, in spite of the war; my work on haematemesis led to some work on shock, particularly that from burns; and in 1942, before going into the Royal Army Medical Corps, I spent eight months in Cambridge with R A McCance and Elsie Widdowson working on water deprivation — a kind of companion piece to the work on salt depletion which they had done at King's College years earlier, and which McCance described in his Goulstonian lecture. (Many years later, as a "water subject," I had the opportunity of comparing notes with David Whitteridge, who had been a "salt subject.") At that time our soldiers were being stranded in damaged tanks in the desert, and our sailors on life rafts. There was temptation for the soldiers to slake their thirst by drinking urine, and for the sailors to drink sea water. The first of these would make the kidneys do over again

5

work which they had already done; the second of these imposed on the kidneys a task of concentration beyond their powers. Our experiments put these insights of common sense on a quantitative basis; concordance with common sense is not incompatible with scientific merit.

At the end of 1942 I joined the RAMC, which brought a doubling of my salary and a certain diminution in medical status. This was brought home to me in the context of an early posting to the camp reception station in Cambridge; a CRS was the army equivalent of a cottage hospital, and only a month or two earlier I had been seeing patients referred from it in the Addenbrooke's outpatient clinic. However, when I reported to the ADMS (assistant director of medical services), he asked me only one question: "How long have you been in the army?" When I said, "Three months," he looked disappointed, and giving me no opportunity to reply, he enlarged on the responsibility of the posting allotted to me, and my obvious lack of fitness for it. He then posted me to a tank regiment at Thetford, where my undergraduate experience of bridge was more relevant than my hard won higher qualifications of MD, MRCP. After a short time I moved on to a field ambulance in the David Copperfield country in the triangle of Norwich, Yarmouth, and Lowestoft, where I acquired another useless accomplishment by learning to ride a motor cycle along the five miles of the Acle straight. The recruiting slogan, "Join the army and see the world" now began to take effect, my first overseas posting being to Sierra Leone. We went out on an American banana boat, the USS *Siboney*, which provided two meals a day, at 7 am and 5 pm, taken standing up, no doubt as a preparation for the exigencies of active service. Not having seen white bread for about three years, we marvelled at this unhealthy luxury.

When we berthed at Freetown the west Africans, whom we then called "natives," came round the ship, and their language soon made us aware that our exports had not been limited to the gospel and to firewater. The west African hospital to which we were posted was in a place called Grafton Valley, a few miles away from the coast, and still in the bush. The first night we were there one of the Africans killed a green mamba, but that was the last snake I was to see till we reached India. The roads in Sierra Leone, being made of iron-containing laterite, were bright red; this gave a good opportunity for chameleons to emerge from the bush as a streak of green, and re-enter it as a streak of red. After a couple of months in this tropical cul de sac we returned to Freetown. We liked the look of the ship in the harbour, the *Britannic*, and we were to be on it for the next two months, including a week in Durban harbour. When we got to Bombay there was the engaging sight of our African soldiers selling their issue cigarettes — known as "Bicycles," of unknown origin — to the Indians. I suppose a sale of cigarettes was better than a gift of bilharzia; but not much.

From Bombay our hospital went up to a place in the Deccan called Dhond, about 40 miles east of Poona; and we spent about nine months there, during which I played chess with Wilfrid Card, who later became a pioneer of mathematics applied to medicine; he always won. I also had an attack of serum hepatitis, probably the sequel to a yellow fever vaccination three months earlier. Somewhere in the *Republic* Plato suggests that the best doctor is the one who has had most diseases himself; and within limits this is not a bad principle, as we should know what it is like to be a patient. I had gone in for puzzling illnesses — as a medical student I had had shingles, in which the pain comes on a day or two before the rash gives the answer; and now, with the hepatitis, a very unfamiliar lack of appetite preceded either darkening of the urine or yellowing of the skin.

If you are puzzled by a military hospital not admitting a single patient for many months while a world war was raging, put it down to the excellence of military security — in India they thought we were still in west Africa; and in west Africa they didn't miss us. Our regular colonel was very content to have all the stores in a single tent and not dispersed through a working hospital, from which they might disappear unaccountably. But we were discovered at last, and sent on our way to Burma via Ranchi and Chittagong.

Only a few weeks later I retraced my steps, obeying a summons to take charge of the biochemistry division of the Central Military Pathology Laboratory back in Poona. Neither ignorance of biochemistry nor basic qualifications in clinical medicine were any excuse, so for the next couple of years I contemplated sprue in the company of Paul Fourman, Jimmy Robinson, now of Dunedin, and Jim Robson, now of Edinburgh. In the hot weather we found it comfortable in the laboratory to work stripped to the waist; but one day Paul and I were caught by the regular colonel, who pointed out that if a messenger came in with a specimen he would not know if we were officers. Paul's offer to have crowns tattooed on our shoulders did not help, and from what we now know of tattooing it would have been a mistake. (The only formal reprimand that I received in the army came from something quite different. While we were still in west Africa one of the troops who was unfamiliar with the thermometer bit the end of it off when the orderly put it in his mouth, and fortunately spat it out. But the thermometer was the only one we had got, and it had become distinctly unserviceable. I asked how to replace it, and was told there were two methods. The simpler one was to send someone in to Freetown with a shilling, and this would produce a thermometer that day. The alternative was to fill in a certificate of accidental loss or breakage, together with a requisition form, and send it up the line; if nothing went wrong this might produce a thermometer within the month. Being an impatient character I chose the first method, which worked; and I thought no more about it. Months later, and by then in India, I was confronted with the record of my misdemeanour in bypassing the proper channels; fortunately, my explanation was accepted, subject to no repetition of such an offence.)

Before this prologue becomes a chronicle, I must hurry on. I returned to England in 1946, to be met by the omen of a dock strike in Southampton, and a posting to Hamburg, which of course lay in ruins at that time. I completed my military service at roughly the same time as my brown shoes wore out; and I re-entered the civilian world resplendent in a demob suit. I had applied for the post of lecturer in medicine in Manchester, where Robert Platt had just taken up the first full time chair of medicine; I had met him in India, and he knew something of the work that I had done on kidney function in patients with haematemesis. I had never been to Manchester, and as the train made a halting progress through Stockport, Levenshulme, and Ardwick my memories of St Andrews, Oxford, Cambridge, and even Poona took on a retrospective glow. Nevertheless, I was very glad to get a post in a new developing unit.

In those days, it was a common thing for posts as lecturer to be held for one or two years by people who did not intend to follow the academic path, but were waiting for a post on the staff of a hospital to crop up. I had been in Manchester for about a year when I met the dean, William Brockbank, in the corridor. In later years I got to know William as the kindest of men but he was physically rather overpowering, and I was slightly taken aback by his question, "How long are you staying in Manchester?" When in doubt, tell the truth — much safer than any alternative. So I replied, "I don't know." If either of us had known that the answer was to be 26 years we might have been surprised. In later chapters I shall have much to say, under various headings, of my experiences in the city where I spent the greater part of my professional life. For the immediate purpose, however, it may be enough to say that when Robert Platt resigned his headship of the department on his election to the presidency of the Royal College of Physicians, I was chosen to succeed him, and took up post as professor at the beginning of 1959.

A pawnbroker has only three balls to deal with, and they are static; but a professor of medicine has to juggle with four — practice, teaching, research, and administration — and they are constantly changing. In addition, a professorial chair seems to act as some kind of magnet for national commitments of various kinds. Academic theory dictates that in the interests of academic mobility every effort should be made to attract a candidate from the ends of the earth, preferably bringing with him a new discipline. Almost always in these hard times such a theory is overset by practicality, since few university departments can now afford a complete change of emphasis and the consequent replacement of equipment. But in the late 'fifties universities were less constrained, and my own university had a good look round before it fell back on me. It is typical of Manchester University that, when a decision had been reached, the vice chancellor, Sir William Mansfield Cooper, came to my room to tell me himself. I think I was so overcome by long delayed euphoria as to tell him that I thought they had made a sensible choice; he seemed in need of reassurance, and of course that is something that should come naturally to the practising doctor which I then was.

Leaving aside any consideration of personality, I actually do believe that a professor appointed from within the same hospital has got certain advantages to set against those which might attend the bringing in of new blood. Having worked in the same hospital for some years, he knows which of his colleagues are both helpful and appropriately knowledgeable ; and, just as important, he knows the minority who are deficient in either one of those attributes. To pursue what may be a rationalisation a little further, it may be possible for an internally appointed professor to accept national commitments somewhat earlier than would be wise for someone who had to learn the ways of an unfamiliar hospital, and also build up a department virtually from scratch.

Be that as it may, after a few years I found myself heavily occupied with external examining — an important way of learning from one's colleagues — and also with membership of the Medical Research Council. Again, I shall have much to say about research and its administration later on; but after the normal four year stint (1966-70), I was recalled to take the chair of the clinical research board in 1971. During the next two years the board structure of the MRC was radically altered, and the arrangements for governmental support of research were the subject of a controversy associated, perhaps unfairly, with a trenchant paper produced by Lord Rothschild. In 1973 I moved from the university world into the civil service, as chief scientist in the Department of Health and Social Security; but I went in on secondment, not daring to emulate stout Cortez in burning my boats. Four years later, on the Monday after Palm Sunday in 1977, I was elected president of the Royal College of Physicians, and was thus able — more fortunate than Caesar — to recross the Rubicon.

As a young man, I believed in the value of personal academic mobility, by which I mean changing one's occupation, or at least one's post, at intervals before becoming stale. This becomes more difficult in an established post; and I count myself very fortunate, and not a little surprised, that in the past decade I have once again been able to enjoy the refreshment that comes from new challenges. When I come to my next chapter, on the practice of medicine, in spite of the sorrow, ignorance, and frustration that all doctors suffer from time to time, I hope to be able to bring out also the interest and challenge of medical life, and the great rewards that it brings. I have been greatly fortunate in pursuing an occupation which has given me much more pleasure than pain; which has been well rewarded not only in material terms; and which has continued to occupy me well into retirement.

2 The practice of medicine

If I were writing a textbook of medicine I would no doubt begin with the theoretical aspects. But since I am not — and no doubt that is a good thing for all of us — I will devote my first substantive chapter to my memories of individual medical practice. And for doing so I can find a warrant in the words of R L Stevenson:

"Perhaps there is no subject on which a man should speak so gravely, as on that industry, whatever it may be, which is the occupation or delight of his life; which is his tool to earn or serve with; and which, if it be unworthy, stamps itself as a mere incubus of dumb and greedy bowels on the shoulders of labouring humanity."

We doctors are, on those terms, fortunate in two ways. Amid some criticism of our methods and of our results, I do not think that many would stigmatise the aims of medicine as unworthy. And the actual practice of medicine, while mainly an absorbing occupation, can also surprisingly carry overtones of delight, derived in the main from our privileged contact with all sorts and conditions of men. (Of course, when I speak in general terms of "men," I have in mind the good Scotch phrase, "Men embrace women.")

There might perhaps be more question on the emphasis that I have placed on individual medical practice. Siren voices, and also some rather raucous ones, tell us that the business of doctors is not to look after the sick but to keep people healthy. This view has found expression in some rather striking phrases, for example the description of the national health service as an "ill health service"; or the professed aim of the World Health Organisation as "Health for all by the year 2000." Since most healthy people want to stay that way (and indeed the lack of such a wish may itself be a sign of ill health), the positive half of the attitude is appealing, and I accept it without question. Doctors should have a real concern for the general health not only of the community in which they live, but for all mankind; and my admiration knows no bounds for people such as Halfdan Mahler, Denis Burkitt, and Richard Doll whose work and concern have made practical contributions to the health of millions. But if one looks at the negative side of the proposition — "not to look after the sick" — I believe it stands revealed as a dangerous half truth. A half truth, or false antithesis, because it is biased towards a collectivist, and away from an individualist, approach; and dangerous, because in the thinking of politicians it may be made the excuse for underfunding both the services on which today's invalids depend and medical research, which may either prevent or alleviate tomorrow's illness.

These beliefs of mine may perhaps be a rationalisation, to justify the things to which I have paid most attention in my own professional life; on the other hand, they may just conceivably be well based — and, at the pragmatic level, caring for sick people is what most doctors do. Prediction is said to be hazardous, but my guess is that doctors will be doing much the same in the years 2000 and 3000, provided of course that they have not either been plunged into or stumbled into the horrors of nuclear, chemical, or even a general conventional war.

One final point, before I pass with some relief from the general to the particular. I have spent the greater part of my life in the academic world, including 26 years in the University of Manchester. It is at times suggested that such an environment effectively precludes any contact with the real world. At least in medicine, this is not only nonsense, it is demonstrable nonsense. The patients whom an academic doctor sees in the outpatient clinic and in the wards are real patients; they suffer from common as well as from rare diseases, and indeed do so, as might be expected, more commonly; and he is as much responsible for them, at the appropriate level, as any other doctor. Like other doctors', our personal contact with patients is less continuous and directly caring than that of our sister profession of nursing; but in the academic sphere we are more fortunate than they, in that teaching and practice can continue to the highest levels in combination, rather than be separated at an early stage of a career. Nor do I think that the quality of clinical practice is in any way impaired either by carrying it out among critical colleagues, or having to explain it to intelligent and inquiring students. After that over protesting, but I suspect necessary, piece of justification let me now try to express, through particular examples, what medical practice has meant to me, from the time when I began it well before the NHS was started, to the time when I gave it up some 40 years later.

Most of the people, including doctors, who read this may have to be reminded that in the 1930s there was widespread poverty and unemployment, and that the services of family doctors were available as on a "free" basis only to those covered by health insurance, which generally meant male employees. General practitioner services for children, women, and the elderly, as well as for the self employed, had to be paid for. This was brought home to me very clearly when, as a demonstrator in pathology at a salary of £50 a year, I was eking this out by doing a weekend locum in general practice. A Dundee jute worker in his early 60s, but looking at least 10 years older, came into the evening surgery, blue and coughing with chronic bronchitis. I was able to decipher from his scanty notes that he had been on what was then called a "stimulant expectorant" for 10 years; and the purpose of his visit was to collect his bottle of cough medicine, for which he was to pay a half crown (for younger readers, $12\frac{1}{2}$p — not much in comparison with today's prescription charges, but in those days not negligible). A stronger character would no doubt have explained to him that the bottle was probably not doing him much good, taking 10 minutes to do so; a richer man, or perhaps a kinder one, might have paid the half crown himself. But as a young locum, I could scarcely undermine whatever confidence the old man felt in his professional care from his own doctor. So I accepted the situation, but not without feeling demeaned by the whole affair, and also pitying the patient. That experience may have been the emotional root of my eager acceptance of the NHS when it was brought about some years later.

In contrast to the present day, when general practice is a favoured option among some of the best graduates, it could happen that a marginal graduate would go straight into general practice, and begin to earn much more than the £50 a year salary of the resident posts for which his fellow graduates had been selected. I remember, as a hospital resident, receiving an admission note from a fellow student already in practice, which illuminated the problem of a man of 60 with the statement, "Fontanelle closed" — something that normally happens towards the end of infancy, and thus not of great relevance to his present condition.

But most of the newly qualified doctors, whether they meant to work in hospital or in family practice, did spend six months or a year in a resident post in hospital. At that time there were three main types of hospital: the voluntary hospitals, many of them associated with medical schools, and then called teaching hospitals; the municipal hospitals, financed by local government; and a large number of cottage hospitals mainly staffed by local family doctors. There were also private nursing homes, in which a good deal of general and gynaecological surgery was carried out, usually by specialists from the teaching hospitals who received only a small honorarium for their hospital work and had to depend for their main income on private practice. Then as now, it was easier for the family doctor to recognise when he needed the help of a surgeon than when he needed the advice of a physician. Moreover, the opportunities for critical intervention by a physician were then much fewer, and the complexities of modern therapeutics had scarcely begun.

In consequence of these various factors there were far fewer specialist physicians than surgeons; they were limited to the larger centres, where the need for them was sufficiently manifest to enable them to earn a living — not of course comparable to the surgeon-princes of the day, but enough to qualify them for the status of the "decent poor," between the family doctor above and the clergyman below. Even in the teaching hospitals some of the posts as "physician" were held by family doctors. From the shelter of the teaching hospital, in my case the Dundee Royal Infirmary, what lay outside looked distinctly chaotic, and it certainly did little to whet my appetite for a career in what Alwyn Smith suggests should be called "commercial medicine." I have, of course, learnt since that both in this country and in the United States medical care paid for in the private sector by those who can afford it is compatible with the highest professional standards, and patients are entitled to seek it; but payment in itself does not guarantee good treatment, still less a favourable outcome.

I shall return later to the dramatic changes in medical practice brought about by the pharmacological revolution, and by the provision of the NHS. But in the meantime, what was it like to be a resident in 1936? The most dramatic change in a doctor's professional life takes place when the final year medical student, weighed down by much information but little practised in using it, passes an examination, has a brief holiday, and finds himself not only seeing patients — that he has done before — but actually having to take decisions about them, decisions which may be of life and death importance. For myself, I think I was too busy to be introspective; but I have had many opportunities since to see how the young man or woman whom you met, nervous and depressed, in the final examination, becomes rejuvenated in a few short weeks of actual responsibility. After five or six years' training you are impatient to make some practical use of it; and I expect that today's young graduates feel much as we did. There are, however, some differences between the resident post then and now.

In those days the staff of a medical unit consisted of a physician, an assistant physician, and possibly a clinical assistant who was also in general practice. Below these, with an aching void between, came the house physician —

the full time paid junior hospital doctor had not been invented. The physician did a daily ward round, seeing every patient and having the final say in all decisions; but he certainly expected to be given the information about the patient on which to base them. I worked for Professor Adam Patrick, whose former house physicians can all be recognised by a callosity on the writing finger of the right hand. A full history and examination of all patients admitted was expected for the morning ward round. On the other hand, the investigative avalanche still lay unperceived on the mountainside above us. The work was perhaps much more clinical, in the sense of spending time with patients, than it is now; and the absence of junior colleagues with whom to discuss problems, while in the main a disadvantage, at least saved time that might have been spent in embroidering the obvious, or poring over investigations whose rationale lay solely in the capacity of the laboratory to perform them (our very limited clinical laboratory closed down at 5 pm, and the advice, so often given, to avoid unnecessary tests is powerfully reinforced by awareness that you will have to do them yourself, in time salvaged from other pressing tasks).

There is another difference between the work of a resident then and now, which should be remembered by any senior physician who criticises today's house physicians for their demands for such things as study leave, holidays, and payments for overtime. While the responsibility of the post has not increased, and may even have been diluted by the availability of advice from junior colleagues, the complexity and intensity of the task have certainly increased. To put it in more concrete terms, in the past, if a patient died in the night the resident was wakened by the night sister, shambled to the ward to see the body, signed a somnambulist death certificate, and retired to bed. His present day successor may well be called at an earlier stage of a crisis, spend some hours in intensive care, have perhaps to estimate, and certainly to consider, biochemical findings — and perhaps at the end of the road still have a death certificate to sign. In spite of all this, I am happy to say that the resilience of youth still operates to prevent today's young doctors from giving way to the vapours.

However much the details of a house physician's work may have changed, I suspect that the main thing that he has to learn at this stage remains the same. During his time as a student he should already have learnt how to talk to patients, and to sympathise with them in their lot. But there is a further skill which is difficult to acquire except under the direct stimulus of responsibility for practical decision — I mean the skill of knowing when a patient is really ill, by which I mean has an illness of sufficient gravity to justify undertaking treatment or imposing restrictions (for example bed rest) that are likely to be unwelcome. This is not a skill that can be put into words, given the variability both of disease and of a patient's reaction to it; but a good doctor acquires it, mainly in the casualty department and to some extent by trial and error. To begin with, it may be sensible to admit too many patients rather than too few, even on the pragmatic ground that an unnecessary admission will either be pointed out to you, or otherwise become apparent, whereas you may never know of patients whom you should have admitted, but did not.

My use in this context of the term really ill should not make you believe that I share the view, which is sometimes expressed, that doctors are besieged by hordes of patients asking attention for trivial illness. The very term trivial illness reminds me of Robert Platt's definition of a minor operation as "an operation done on someone else." To visit a doctor or a hospital is not so pleasant an experience as to be easily undertaken by someone who does not have a problem. Even if the problem amounts to little more than a worry in the mind, it is still a problem. There may be the occasional patient who becomes addicted to doctors, or even one doctor; but where there is actual evidence, for example from the General Household Survey, it shows that the great bulk of illness is cared for domestically or in the community, without medical intervention. The family doctor, at the end of a busy surgery, may not see things quite in

that way — but after all he can count only those who have
come to see him, and not the larger number who have
coped without his help.

But it is high time I followed the moving finger to the
next phase of my career, which was supported financially
by a research fellowship from the Medical Research Council
and the Beit Memorial Trust, and was spent mainly in
Oxford, at the Radcliffe Infirmary. I did some research, as
was proper in the holder of a research fellowship; but it is
understood that a clinical research fellow must also maintain
a degree of clinical competence. This I did in two ways: by
being a registrar to Dr A M Cooke (later to become a most
esteemed friend); and by spending many mornings in the
outpatient clinic, particularly during the early war years
when the population increased and the number of available
physicians diminished.

The honorary post as registrar with Alex Cooke entailed
accompanying him on his ward rounds, which gave me a
liberal education, and writing summaries of his patients on
discharge. Having mastered the art of writing voluminous
primary records on patients, it was a useful additional
discipline to have to boil down someone else's notes so that
they could survive the scrutiny of a master of a language
which happily is common to Scotland and England, even if
somewhat less so to America.

In the outpatient clinic I greatly enlarged my experience
both of patients and of disease. The patients were a fasci-
nating blend of rustics from the Cotswolds, emigré cockneys
from the town, and students and teachers from the gown. I
suspect that my patients had as much difficulty with my
Scotch accent as I had with their varied ones; I even have
evidence to support this from a colleague who told me that
a patient had said to him, "I find it difficult to understand
the German doctor I saw last time." Since there were not
too many German doctors in Oxford at the time, he looked
at the notes and recognised my writing.

It was at this time too that I became aware that intelligence gives little or no protection against the upsetting effect
of illness. Oxford is known to contain intelligent people,

some of them actually in the university (or "Oxford College," as it was known to tourists asking the way). But when they became ill both common sense and high intelligence seemed to desert them — their faculties were benumbed, like those of Tom Birch when he took pen in hand. It was disconcerting to discover that a world authority on, say, Coptic was incapable, under the stress of illness, of giving consistent answers to simple questions. I also met another phenomenon, superficially similar, but different in cause: the lesser English public schools provide a veneer which inspires confidence but may be a thin layer masking an intellectual chasm. Again, I acknowledge that the public school system at its best has great merits; but it must have something to work on. I share the preference or prejudice, in another context, of Oliver Cromwell, who wrote: "I had rather have a plain russet-coated Captain that knows what he fights for, and loves what he knows, than that which you call 'a Gentleman', and is nothing else. I honour a *Gentleman* that is so indeed."

At the practical level of obtaining a medical history, and later on of discussing the illness with the patient, one's conversation should be plain, even if the patient appears to possess a wide vocabulary; for he may either be an intelligent man perplexed by illness, or even a relatively dull or prejudiced person who has been educated beyond his intellectual means. Let me hasten to say that the same considerations apply to doctors when they become patients.

My four years in the army gave an opportunity for whatever burgeoning clinical talent I may have had to lie fallow. For, as I have mentioned, I spent the first months of my service either in recurrent transit or else attached to a hospital that was not open, and for the rest of the time I was in charge of the biochemical division of the Central Military Pathology Laboratory in Poona. While there I kept in touch with medical advances through the weekly journals, but any survey of the "medical literature" entailed a journey of just over 100 miles to the Haffkine Institute in Bombay. The shelves containing bound volumes of the *Journal of Physiology* were next to the glass cases containing the snakes from which venom was obtained for the preparation of antivenom. It is not so easy to lose oneself in a physiological paper as in a novel, but it can happen, and the hiss of an angry viper and its strike against the glass make an unpleasant end to a reverie. For all the great interest of pathology, and the many splendid colleagues who practise that branch of medicine, I found that my appetite for clinical work could not be satisfied merely by attending clinical meetings, or by doing research on sprue. The first of these activities lacked the salt of actual responsibility, the second lacked the variety of a general clinical commitment. I was therefore glad to return home, and fortunate to be appointed as lecturer in the new full time department of medicine in Manchester.

A clinical academic appointment entails responsibility for teaching, research, and some administration, but the holder of such a post must also be clinically competent, though not necessarily outstanding. He cannot teach clinical medicine without practising it, and he must enjoy the respect of clinical colleagues outside the academic fold. Because of his academic duties he is likely to have less time to spend in clinical work; but the patients whom he sees are still real, and have a right to quality in care. After four years away from clinical work, and entering a hospital in which I had never worked before, I felt strange for a time. But it soon wore off, thanks to a chief of superlative clinical skills in Robert Platt, the friendliest set of colleagues I have ever known, and above all plenty of inescapable clinical opportunity. The health service was still two years distant, the hospital was surrounded by a much denser population than now remains, and there was open access to the outpatient department. Although I had done several clinics each week in wartime Oxford, they were leisurely affairs with perhaps a half dozen new patients in the morning. At the Manchester Royal Infirmary the general medical clinic began at 9 30 am and seldom finished before 3 pm. The doctors at least had a cup of coffee and a biscuit during this time, but the unfortunate patients might wait for several hours and might not be able to afford a snack. Even after the health service

21

began it was some years before an appointment system was established. As a service to patients the old fashioned clinic could not be condoned, but as a sink or swim course for a doctor in need of clinical rehabilitation it could scarcely have been equalled.

Somewhat paradoxically, I always preferred the outpatient clinic to the wards for clinical work, but for teaching my preference was the reverse. The advantages of teamwork in the service of patients are well recognised and acknowledged; diagnosis and treatment can be thoroughly discussed, and mistakes thereby prevented. But for the satisfaction of the instinct to solve a clinical problem the cluttered ward round, in which each patient has already told his story to two or three people, does not compare with the first visit of the patient to the hospital doctor. It might be an exaggeration to say that the first history is always the best, but it certainly is the freshest. When it comes to teaching, however, there is a certain conflict of interest between the patient and the students. The essence of an outpatient visit should be the history and examination carried out by the consultant or his deputy; this process is not greatly disturbed by the presence of one or two students, and it is important for them to see and hear a consultation in progress. It is also valuable for the students to hear the preliminary clinical assessment and how this is communicated to the patient. But the occasional student, on hearing mention of a possible illness, may display an appetite for hearing the sort of disquisition on it which might constitute the answer to a question in an examination. This is not a reasonable request in a busy clinic, and would of course be particularly inappropriate in the presence of a patient. Another corruption of the value of the outpatient clinic, particularly for the patient, is when the clinic room is converted into a lecture theatre for the display of the consultant's histrionic ability before an entire class of students. The outpatient consultation, ideally perhaps a tête-à-tête, can withstand the addition of a couple of students, but to convert it into a class exercise amounts to a distortion.

On the other hand, the ward, or a side room attached to

it, makes the ideal setting for clinical teaching. The patient is well known to the teacher, he has become familiar with the hospital, investigations have been done, and his consent to being discussed with students can be truly informed, and not just a casual answer to a question during booking for a clinic. Some patients actually enjoy being taught on, but this is more likely to be so in the ward, where they are likely to have already met the teacher, than in the outpatient clinic, where everything is strange and may even appear hostile. Most patients probably do not greatly enjoy exposure to a class of students, but nevertheless are willing to accept it as a social duty. There is a minority of patients who are plainly upset at the prospect of appearing before a class, and they should not be made the victims of persuasion.

Manchester is a cosmopolitan city, but the greater part of outpatients were native Lancastrians. I cannot speak too highly of them. They are notably humorous, a stock from which famous comedians have come; they are also down to earth and full of common sense, but they lack the hardness of some of the folk across the Pennines, without in any way being pushovers. Before consumerism was invented, Lancashire people were often more honest with their customers than might have been wished by their employers. My wife has been more than once advised in a shop that some items were past their best. And on one occasion in the university refectory, a senior waitress, Mrs Harris, warned the professor of clinical surgery that a "special" dish would cost him five old pence more. At that time John Morley was not impoverished, and was indeed wont to express regret that as a successful surgeon he was not able to hand on to his children the advantages of poverty and culture that he had enjoyed as the son of a clergyman.

Every patient is interesting, if not for a disease which may be quite mundane, then for himself. Occasionally you meet a descendant of some great man. Once in Manchester, seeing the unusual name Gresham on the front sheet of the notes, I asked the patient whether he was descended from the originator of Gresham's law —and he was, though the dozen or so intervening generations must have subjected the

23

original genome to near homoeopathic dilution. In other contexts, I have met a descendant of Thomas Linacre, who founded the Royal College of Physicians in 1518; and coming nearer to our own day, a grand-daughter of Sigmund Freud. Coming back for a moment to Gresham's law, which asserts that bad money drives out good, I have sometimes fancied an analogy with the way in which, faced with a difficult task to be done, or even a blank page seeking to be filled, we seize on any trivial occupation of a routine and undemanding nature to postpone the moment of truth.

One of the most obvious changes in medicine over the past 50 years has been the increase in specialisation. Within the surgical specialties, this has been based on technical skills as well as an increase in a defined body of knowledge. The first of these factors has been less conspicuous in medicine until fairly recently, although now the advent of endoscopy has had a major influence on the practice of medical gastroenterology, and renal biopsy on nephrology. Specialisation has been at different times both the cause and the result of dramatic increases in what can be done for patients with particular conditions. This has had repercussions both on the way in which hospital practice is organised, and on the capacity of the individual physician.

To take the organisational aspects first, 50 years ago the majority of physicians even in a teaching hospital were "general," in the sense that they would be willing (and competent) to give a considered view on the whole range of internal medicine as then understood. The hospital clinics were correspondingly known as general outpatient clinics. There were also, however, a few clinics devoted to special conditions such as diabetes, but mostly these were staffed by physicians who would still claim to be general. Perhaps the first group to limit their scope to a single branch of internal medicine were the neurologists; and they have been followed at intervals by cardiologists, gastroenterologists, and many others. Even when general medical clinics remain, the patients sent to them no longer cover the whole range of internal medicine, for the family doctors will quite properly have referred many types of patient to the more specialised clinics. The situation in a district hospital remains somewhat different, for there are far fewer physicians on the staff of any one hospital; each of them may have a special interest, but there cannot be the multiplicity of clinics found in a larger hospital.

For the individual physician this tendency towards greater specialisation has important consequences, and indeed brings some tensions during training. He does not know initially whether his ultimate career is to be in a teaching centre or in a district hospital. If the former, he may need greater emphasis on acquiring knowledge and experience in a specialty; if the latter, there is a greater need to conserve the general skills of a physician, so that he may be capable of bearing his share of the general medical commitment of a district hospital. Another consequence for the individual physician of the vast expansion of useful medical knowledge is that he can no longer (if he ever could) expect to cope single handed with all that is necessary to help his patients. The most obvious result of this is perhaps the development of medical "firms" or teams, in which consultants work with one or more consultant colleagues and also with so called junior doctors, who may be in their late 30s, and who may well, whatever their age, be better informed on particular aspects of a problem than their more generalised chief. Furthermore, no team, however large, can hope to cope with all aspects of any problem, and each physician must build up a system of consultation with colleagues.

The development of specialties centred on the various systems of the body (circulatory, respiratory, nervous, etc) has also led to closer cooperation between physicians and surgeons with a common interest in a particular system. Finally, it is quite important for any practising doctor to keep abreast, in a general way, with advances in specialties other than his own; if he does not do this he may find himself prejudicing patients by warning them off procedures which were hazardous in his student days of 30 and more years ago, but have since been made safe, and indeed desirable, by advances made by other men in other places.

Like other physicians, I had a special interest, which

developed through studies of body fluid into the study of medical disorders of the kidney, known as nephrology. Advanced disease of the kidneys brings harmful consequences to almost every system of the body — high blood pressure, anaemia, vomiting and diarrhoea, breathlessness, heart failure, bone disease, convulsions, and coma. Whether because of this, or as a rationalisation based on it, nephrologists took longer to peel off from the general body of physicians than some other organ centred specialists. The separation of specialties may be a slow gradual process, brought about by steady increase in knowledge, or it may happen more rapidly, stimulated by either an important new diagnostic procedure or by a new and effective form of treatment. In nephrology both these things happened. The development of a safe technique for getting small samples of kidney tissue through a needle enabled different types of kidney disease to be distinguished during life, and appropriate management to be undertaken. At about the same time, the development of a permanent Teflon shunt between artery and vein by Belding Scribner in Seattle paved the way for long term dialysis of patients in renal failure. Dialysis had of course been practised before Scribner, most notably by Willem Kolff in wartime Holland, but it was a one off affair, appropriate for treating acute reversible renal failure but not for chronic dialysis. Repeated access to the circulation, made possible by Scribner's work, and of course developed in various ways since then, opened the way to long term dialysis as a practical method of treatment for terminal renal failure. It also greatly increased the chances of survival after renal transplantation by covering the interval during which the transplanted kidney was not yet functioning effectively after suffering the inevitable period during which it had been deprived of circulating blood.

Like so many other advances in medicine, the possibility of substituting for damaged kidney function has brought difficult ethical problems of selection. The balance between dietary measures, haemodialysis, peritoneal dialysis, and renal transplantation remains a major preoccupation for today's nephrologists. However, my voice from the past seeks to remind them that such problems are at any rate an advance on the previous situation, in which there was nothing effective to be done for a patient in terminal renal failure other than relief of symptoms. I can well remember the anxiety of watching patients with reversible acute renal failure, who passed little or no urine for an uncertain number of days, during which they naturally became iller and iller, and would of course die if renal function did not recover sufficiently or in time. Such a situation could arise after a mismatched transfusion, a period of circulatory collapse, or a back street abortion. Nowadays, such patients can be kept alive and relatively well by one or more episodes of dialysis until the damaged kidneys renew their function.

Even worse than the anxiety of awaiting the resumption of an adequate flow of urine in acute renal failure was the sadness of seeing patients with irreversible loss of kidney function from chronic renal disease, and knowing that their end was inevitable and near. One experience that emphasised for me the importance of communication arose in this context. I was explaining to the relatives of one such patient that the outlook was hopeless, and that the last few days were likely to be unpleasant, at least until the patient became unconscious; and I was a little surprised to see that they were not looking at me, but gazing rather fixedly at a book on my desk. Following their gaze, I saw that they must have been reading the title of the book, which was *How to Learn Medicine*.

This taught me to be more careful, not only about what I said but about the ambience in which I said it. Not only can evil communications corrupt good manners, they can also vitiate the very best medicine; and we owe a great debt to Charles Fletcher, who in his Rock Carling lecture and at other times has kept before us the importance of communication, which includes talking with as well as talking to patients. I am not entirely convinced of the value of set courses in communication, and would rather place a general obligation on medical teachers to emphasise, and above all to illustrate, the value of good communication, each in his own context. I was rather horrified recently to come, in a draft, on the statement, "Doctors should learn from practitioners of alternative medicine how to talk to patients." I felt that this should be amended to, "Doctors should not have to learn from practitioners of alternative medicine how to talk to patients."

Like any doctor who has spent the greater part of his life in practice, I am deeply conscious of how much I owe to the patients with whom I have shared either the gladness of recovery or the sadness of ill health; and also to the colleagues with whom I have shared so many discussions, and from whom I have learnt so much. In my case, this was largely by listening to them, unlike an occasion described to me by Robert Platt who, as a relatively new professor of medicine in Manchester, was visited by Stanley Davidson, a veteran of Aberdeen and later of Edinburgh, and a man of copious eloquence. According to Robert, Stanley Davidson came into his office at the appointed time, sat down, talked for an hour or so without interruption, looked at his watch, and got up to go with the parting words, "Thank you, Platt, I've learnt a great deal from our talk."

I count myself very fortunate that I have now been qualified for a period of 50 years which has seen a general improvement in the public health —partly of course due to social and environmental factors —and also a great improvement in the prospects for cure of individual patients suffering from a wide spectrum of diseases that were incurable half a century ago. A host of detailed causes underlie these improvements; but in this country at least, two things stand out: the advances in medical knowledge, and the availability of medical care through the National Health Service. In the next chapter I shall describe my impressions mainly as a spectator, but in minor degree as a participant, in these important processes.

3 The progress of medicine

The theme of this chapter is that there has been an improvement in the health of individuals and of the population as a whole over the past 50 years; and that while general social factors have certainly contributed to this, it has been largely due to advances in medical scientific knowledge, and to that degree of approach to equity in health care which is represented by the National Health Service. To establish this theme, we need a positive answer to three questions: Has there been an improvement in health? Has increase in medical knowledge contributed to it? Has access to health care improved?

HAS THERE BEEN IMPROVEMENT IN HEALTH?

This is not a judgment that you can make simply by looking around, as one can be naively misled in either direction. I can recall my difficulty in squaring my knowledge that the mean expectation of life among Indians in war time was around 25 years with my observation of large numbers of aged and crippled Indians, an observation that was assisted by the benevolent custom of employing thieves who had become infirm as chowkidars, or night watchmen — a primitive form of protection racket. The explanation was to be found in the tremendously high infant and childhood mortality, which dragged down the curve of survival. Conversely, the much higher, and increasing, expectation of life in developed countries in no way clears our streets of obvious invalids and cripples. A fair answer to the question can come only from the use of objective indices, of which the most categorical must surely be mortality — even in epidemiology "stone dead hath no fellow." Crude mortality figures can be misleading when we are dealing in comparisons over time, as (to be obvious) the age structure of a population changes with fluctuations in birth rate, and at the other extreme with wars and pestilence; and (to be still more obvious) old people are more likely to die within a given period than young people. Nevertheless, when mortality over time is standardised to take account of changes in age structure, a notable fall in mortality becomes apparent. The death rate per 1000 in both men and women is now only about half of what it was in 1931, and this fall in mortality, while greatest in early life, is seen also in advanced age. As Cyril Clarke has pointed out, there has been nearly a tenfold increase in centenarians since 1951, representing an accumulation of increased life expectancy over the decades.

There is of course more to life than simply postponing death, but terms such as well or ill lack the precision of dead or alive. The same degree of objective disability can cause quite different perceptions of illness in different people. The General Household Survey includes questions on health, but the answers lack diagnostic precision. What they do show, as I mentioned in the previous chapter, is that by far the greatest part of perceived illness is not cared for by doctors, whether in the community or in hospital, but is either borne stoically, or treated by lay resources in the neighbourhood. This makes medical surveys of illness a very incomplete reflection of the totality of ill health within a population; but on the other hand they do bring greater diagnostic precision to defining the limited population who actually consult a doctor. Comparisons of morbidity over time are much more uncertain than comparisons of mortality, because of changing incidence of illness, different perceptions of illness, and different attitudes of observers, whether these are lay or medical. I am thus reduced to the personal recollection that in the hungry 'thirties there was more visible medical abnormality in the streets than there is now — with one exception. There is now more disturbed behaviour, as the level of alcohol consumption has gone up, and as some people at one time sheltered in asylums are discharged into the community, unaccompanied by the resources that would assist their re-entry into society. In general terms, however, there is no indication from observations of morbidity to contradict the evidence from mortality statistics that the health of the nation and of individuals has improved.

HAS IMPROVED MEDICAL KNOWLEDGE MADE A CONTRIBUTION?

My personal answer to this question must be Yes, coming as it does from someone who qualified at a time when effective treatment, so far as internal medicine is concerned, was practically limited to insulin, liver extract, and digitalis. But assertion is not enough, and in attempting a reasoned answer I will begin with a frankly personal account of the outstanding things which made me aware that the virtual therapeutic nihilism of my medical teachers was being replaced by a true therapeutic revolution. I shall then mention briefly some more general evidence bearing on the question; and finally address myself to what I cannot help seeing as a paradox: that after all these advances what is called modern or scientific medicine has, after a period of general, and even at times grateful, acceptance, come under criticism of unusual severity, especially in the past decade.

I suppose that if you were to ask a dozen doctors who have been qualified for 50 years what things had impressed them as advances, they would each tell a different tale. I can only, in outline, try to tell you mine. When I qualified, once infection got into the general bloodstream, as septicaemia, it was almost certain to be fatal. A rare personal tragedy would be if a surgeon, or a pathologist doing a postmortem examination, accidentally cut his finger, he was himself liable to die as a result. A much more common, and perhaps even greater tragedy was the deaths of mothers from puerperal sepsis. These things are not easy to forget. To combat them, we gave intravenous injections of a coloured mercurial called mercurochrome; I remember the excitement when prontosil came along, like mercurochrome in colour, but very different in action, as Leonard Colebrook later showed in puerperal fever, using the successor sulphonamides. A few years later, I was working on haematemesis and on the plasma treatment of burn shock in the Nuffield department of medicine, where the first therapeutic injection of penicillin was being given by Charles Fletcher.

My last personal involvement with what has been called the conquest of infection came after the war, when the first trial of streptomycin in tuberculous meningitis was being set up. At that time the idea of controlled trials was relatively new, and the organisation of multicentre trials was even more rudimentary. Robert Platt happened to be away when the letter of invitation to participate came from the Medical Research Council, and I had to make the decision. As it happened, the senior neurologist on whom the bulk of the work would fall was also away — so, not for the last time, I was able to assent to a proposition that would mean more work for others than for myself. So I had a tiny part in the demonstration that a disease, previously a cause of certain death, had become curable if detected in time. And that of course was only a part of the process which has removed tuberculosis from its infamous position as described by John Bunyan: "the Captain of all those men of death that came to take him away was the Consumption."

Of course, those concerned to point out the element of hubris in the phrase that I have just used, the conquest of infection, can legitimately bring up the problem of bacterial resistance, and — more topically — the annoying plasticity of the viruses, which throws up new problems such as AIDS. But to someone like myself, who has seen a 20% mortality from lobar pneumonia in young and previously healthy men and women, there seems more virtue in gratitude for what has been achieved and hope for what may yet be attained by further research than in repining over the real problems that remain or develop.

I have begun with infection, because that represents the major change in what is now possible, compared with our previous impotence; but that is by no means the whole story. When I qualified, manipulation of the endocrine system was limited to somewhat capricious dried thyroid medically, and subtotal thyroidectomy surgically; with Hench and Kendall's work on corticotrophin and cortisone as a stimulant, endocrine manipulation now extends to the thyroid, pituitary, and adrenal glands, and to the gonads. If Jane Austen's adrenal disease was due to tuberculosis, she could have been cured twice over. Within my own special interest, in body fluid and renal disease, there has been fruitful collaboration between physicians and surgeons, as well as with other branches of medicine such as radiology and biochemistry. Lord Moynihan is reported to have said, "We have made surgery safe for the patient; now we must make the patient safe for surgery." Better anaesthetic agents have contributed greatly to this end, but so also have studies of the metabolic response to surgery, leading to more sensible fluid replacement. Acute renal failure often has a surgical, traumatic, or obstetric cause, and collaboration between these disciplines and renal physicians, together of course with dialysis, has greatly improved the outlook. Chronic renal failure is no longer hopeless, but survival depends on the combined efforts of the renal physician and the transplant surgeon, together with nurses and technicians who have mastered the art of dialysis.

It is salutary to recall my own blunders in the discipline in which I was supposed to be expert. I have no doubt committed others of which I am ignorant, but I would score those which I do recall most vividly at 1.5. When oral diuretics first came in, in the somewhat unsatisfactory form of acetazolamide, I wrote a leading article in the *Lancet* expressing the view that they were not reliable enough to replace the well tried mercurials; it must be some time since anyone has given an injection of a mercurial diuretic, the successors to acetazolamide having driven them from the field. I score that blunder as one point. Later, when dialysis began to be practised more widely, I expressed too conservative a view on its future, saying that it would bring many problems of selection. I was, of course, wrong in my first forecast, but I allow that blunder only half a point, as I could not foresee the extent to which safer and more effective renal transplantation would prevent the accumulation of patients with renal failure successfully palliated by dialysis. (A favourite question for assessors on appointments committees is, "What have you done of which you are most proud?" I could never answer it, as what tended to come into mind were blunders like the above.)

These personal recollections take no account of the important advances in medical disciplines with which I am less familiar. For a more general view of the progress that has been made I turn to Paul Beeson, who succeeded Leslie Witts in the Nuffield chair of medicine at Oxford. He compared the possibilities of effective treatment over the whole range of disorders in the first edition of a leading American textbook of medicine, published in 1927, with what was possible in the fourteenth edition, published in 1975. Classifications of disease have changed in detail, but there were 362 conditions common to the two editions. In 1927 there were effective treatments for less than 25 of these, whereas by 1975 half of the 362 diseases were effectively preventable or treatable.

Before turning to some of the criticisms of modern medicine, let me mention two points that are often overlooked. First, effective preventive medicine is based on scientific knowledge just as much as is the medicine applied to the cure or palliation of disease in the individual. This is often forgotten by those who blame the scientific approach for failure to prevent disease. Secondly, even for individuals the benefits of soundly based medicine are not limited to cure or relief of symptoms; they also include the relief of anxiety, both generally and more specifically in the form of reassurance based on a thorough and knowledgeable analysis of possibilities that may in the end be convincingly ruled out. As Walsh McDermott has pointed out, well based

34

reassurance is an important function of the physician, yet it could scarcely be quantified in a cost-benefit analysis.

Like the inheritance of stature, intelligence, and hypertension, criticism of modern medicine is multifactorial. Some, like Ivan Illich, deny any virtue, regarding medicine as a conspiracy against the public, and even looking on the relief of pain as a hindrance to human experience. Those who accept that some benefits have accrued attach a preponderant role to social factors such as good housing, good nutrition giving greater resistance to infection, improved hygiene, and so on; and they regard the strictly medical contribution as marginal. Another line of criticism is that the exercise of scientific medicine tends to make doctors callous; that doctors increase their influence at the expense of the autonomy of the patient; and that technologically based medicine is too expensive. A further suggestion, on which I have already touched, is that doctors in the pursuit of cure are neglecting prevention. I tried to answer some of these criticisms in my Rock Carling lecture of 1984, under the somewhat contrived title, *An Anthology of False Antitheses*, and I shall not repeat the effort here, since polemics are as tedious to write as to read. To answer criticisms of medicine is to be arrogant; to ignore them is to be complacent. By doing first one and then the other, I can enjoy the worst of both worlds. But let me indulge myself with one sentence from my previous attempt: "The true antithesis of 'caring medicine' is not 'scientific medicine,' or 'high technology medicine,' or 'hospital medicine,' or 'academic medicine,' or 'orthodox medicine'"; it is, quite simply, "bad medicine."

There is a fortunate provision in the Roman church that the effectiveness of absolution depends on the sincerity of the penitent and not on the immaculacy of the priest. There is a half analogy here with the medical process — the outcome of any episode of illness depends, nine times out of ten, on what the patient has actually got wrong with him; but for the vital 10% of episodes what the doctor does is critical, and depends more on his competence than on his moral character. In the past both orthodox medicine and

35

alternative medicine have benefited greatly from the frequency with which nature effects a cure; the new thing is that, as Beeson showed, the number of conditions in which what is done can critically affect the outcome is now considerable. It was possible in the past for a cynic to say, "Though there is a great difference between a good and a bad doctor, there is not much difference between a good doctor and no doctor at all." The first of these propositions remains true, but the second is in an increasing number of situations false.

As a bridge between discussing the contribution of advancing medical knowledge and evaluating the contribution of the National Health Service in improving health in this country, let me recall an occasion when the two were brought somewhat incongruously together. Soon after a report appeared on unequal access to health care, I was the second speaker in a debate in which the openers were each supposed to make their case in 15 minutes. My predecessor spent the first 15 minutes on the irrelevance of modern medicine, and then ran on for a further 10 minutes to deplore the inequity of its distribution. My added time for preparation allowed me to work out how best to draw attention to the apparent inconsistency in the first speaker's case.

HAS ACCESS TO HEALTH CARE BEEN IMPROVED BY THE NHS?

Had I felt complacent about the present state of the health service, I would not have agreed to become president of an organisation entitled Health Concern. Like Sir Francis Avery Jones and others, I look back with some nostalgia to the 'fifties and 'sixties, when there was a virtual political consensus that the NHS was a good system of caring for the nation's health, in spite of disputes on party lines over matters such as prescription charges. There is still massive support for the NHS from those who hold the centre in politics; from the great mass of the general public, who after all still depend on it; and, not least important, from those who actually work in it. In parliament, however, the consensus has been greatly reduced, for a number of reasons to which different people would attach different importance. From no misogynistic stance, but rather with surprise at an apparent lack of compassion from members of the reputedly gentler sex, I would ungallantly lay considerable responsibility on two rather different women.

When Barbara Castle was Secretary of State, she gave a very fair wind to the doctrinaire objective of extruding private practice from the NHS. In this way, a shallow interpretation of fairness prejudiced a useful source of revenue for the service; forced consultants to waste time and energy in acquiring facilities for private practice outside the service; and, worst of all, deprived patients in the private sector (which is not illegal) from access to the special facilities found in hospital, and even in many cases from adequate night cover in emergency. In the event, this has been one of the main factors in the expansion of the private sector in recent years, which has converted it from a marginal activity to an important provider of medical care; Mrs Castle's contribution to this could well be marked by a statue in the forecourt of the Cromwell or Wellington Hospital.

My other anti-heroine is, of course, Margaret Thatcher, who was an excellent Secretary of State for Education and Science (the cut in school milk being marginal, even if symptomatic). A heady mixture of monetarism and power has not turned out well for the universities (whose medical faculties contribute considerably to health care) or for the NHS. Charging so called realistic fees to postgraduate students from overseas has cut off selectively what was once a remarkably cheap way of spreading British influence throughout the world. What a politician says during the run up to an election may not be evidence, but when she said, "The health service is safe with us," I felt a twinge of anxiety — no politician had felt it necessary to say this before.

On the other hand, when I hear suggestions that only a

return to socialism can save the health service, and that otherwise it is inevitably doomed, I feel constrained to point out that health concern is not to be equated with health despair; and that our objective should be a return to general support for the service, not a further increase in political polarisation. It is not possible, as some wish, to take the health service out of politics — both the amount of money involved, and the sensitivity of anything to do with health, will keep the health service a major political preoccupation; but we must somehow get away from its annexation by one side or another, and see it once again as a major national asset. We can be helped in doing so if we try to transcend the difficulties of the past decade — marred as it has been in relation to the health service by three reorganisations; by adverse demographic trends, with more elderly people having to be supported by a smaller active population; and by financial stringency with cash limits and the strains imposed by RAWP (the acronym for the fruits of the Resource Allocation Working Party — in Scotland, with greater cunning, they talk of SHARE, derived from Scottish Health Authorities Revenue Equalisation).

I suggest that some comfort may be drawn from comparing even the present state of the health service with what happened in this country before its introduction ; and, secondly, by comparing access to health care here with what still happens even in wealthier countries such as the United States.

HISTORICAL COMPARISONS

I have already mentioned that the national health insurance scheme which preceded the NHS was limited to employees, so that wives and children, and old people of both sexes, were not entitled to free health care. This did not affect the wealthy, who could pay for it; nor did it necessarily affect the very poor, who could be treated charitably in the voluntary hospitals, which were, however, under increasing strain, some of the revenue coming from precarious sources such as flag days and student rag days. As a tin-carrying student, I was made aware of resentment from middle class people who had to pay for their own health care, had to support the national insurance provision through their taxes or employers' contribution, and who were now being asked to contribute to one type of hospital, whereas another type was being provided "off the rates." Of course, the great majority of people of all classes contributed generously, but there was this undercurrent of feeling that for something as important as health a more coherent system would be better. By extending coverage to all members of the population, while still leaving the option of private health care for those who wanted it and could afford it, the National Health Service was to me the most notable fruit of the period of idealism symbolised by the Beveridge report during the war, and the Attlee administration just after it. It was said of Mussolini's Italy that "Whatever is not prohibited is compulsory." It is a great strength of the NHS that it is there for people to use, but they are entirely free to seek alternatives, financial or conceptual.

For those not covered by the pre-NHS system, and indeed even for those who were, there were inequalities of provision which dwarf even the quite noticeable inequalities that are still with us. It is only with qualification that one can admire the "heroism" with which a general practitioner of those days would remove an inflamed appendix on the kitchen table, partly because the family could not afford admission to a nursing home. In the larger centres and in the main hospitals, whether voluntary or municipal, standards were high; but in the smaller local hospitals standards were distinctly variable. At the beginning of the war, in preparation for the anticipated air raids, doctors were being trained in the technique of slow drip blood transfusion, introduced a year or two earlier by Marriott and Kekwick, of the Middlesex Hospital. From the Radcliffe Infirmary, Charles Fletcher and I went on a missionary tour of the neighbouring cottage hospitals to demonstrate the technique. (Medical television programmes in this country owe a great deal to Charles, who became an organiser and presenter of the responsible series, *Your Life in their Hands*. So I cannot resist telling the one occasion on which I have seen him discomposed. In a patient in shock the veins go into spasm, and it may be difficult to force blood into them from the drip set. Pressure can be applied by attaching a blood pressure cuff to the inlet tube and inflating it. Fortunately, we used coloured water not actual blood; for on one occasion, when Charles was demonstrating this, the cork blew out and the fluid poured up his sleeve. After that we wired in the cork on our demonstration set.) As a byproduct of our mission we learnt something of the practice of these hospitals, which were in one of the more prosperous areas of the country; even so it was distinctly patchy. Some of them were fulfilling a useful function in the care of self limiting acute illness and in convalescence; but in others there was a certain amount of over enthusiasm in doctors practising amateur surgery and anaesthesia. The NHS has dramatically improved this situation in at least two distinct ways: it has provided a wide range of specialist services at district hospital level; and it has clarified the respective responsibilities of the general practitioner and the specialist.

The community hospital still has a valuable part to play in the system, but now the family doctor knows that he can call on specialist help in deciding whether more comprehensive facilities are needed. This may indeed be easier in the public than in the private sector, because of the financial toll of a fully equipped private hospital. Even in remote areas it is obviously more convenient to move a patient 15 miles to a district hospital than 100 miles to Aberdeen or Cardiff. What should determine all of these decisions is what is actually wrong with the patient — and only secondarily his circumstances, financial or geographical.

In many ways the general practitioner, who has to see everything, has a more difficult task than the specialist; and the progress which has been made in providing an appropriate training for his task would have been difficult before the advent of the NHS. A training period spent partly in hospital and partly in general practice allows the options for a future career to stay open a little longer. For mature general practitioners, the provision of practice facilities, secretarial and nursing help, and contact with colleagues and postgraduate centres must surely have raised standards, and probably made them more even. The NHS has also maintained the professional tradition that specialists will see only patients who are referred to them by general practitioners. This tradition is sometimes criticised as a trespass on the right of patients to see whomsoever they want. On balance, it is a tradition that helps the patient, as it ensures that he is seen first by someone with general experience, who is also likely to know the available specialists. A patient who makes his own choice of specialist (or for that matter, of alternative practitioner) runs some risk of choosing the wrong branch of medicine on the basis of his self diagnosis, or worse still, falling into the hands of the wrong specialist, even within the right discipline.

Another familiar criticism of the NHS alleges preoccupation with disease and neglect of prevention. Both for doctors and for patients preoccupation with disease is perhaps not too bad a thing; and I have perhaps said enough about it. But the second half of the charge — neglect of prevention — can perhaps be rebutted on historical grounds. Fifty years ago sanitary knowledge was available, but sanitary practice limped far behind in the poorer parts of the community, both urban and rural. Preventive inoculation had got little further than Jenner and Pasteur. Nutrition was largely a matter of vitamins, and the improvement in the staples of diet which was forced on us by the war had not yet taken place (and is now having to be recovered). A relation between way of life and health was largely unsuspected, except perhaps for the abuse of alcohol. Obesity, at least when moderate, was a sign of good living. In my manse, the only deviation from good habits that was condoned was — smoking. (Lucky I was that my father and I both smoked pipes, which had the half merit of being easier to give up than cigarettes).

To digress to my own smoking history, I have given it twice and the occasion on which I resumed it for a time, in the mid-'sixties, is of some interest. I became a member of the Medical Research Council in 1966, and found that more than half the members smoked pipes or cigars. I remember the chairman, Lord Amory, noticing just as an official photograph of the council was about to be taken, that the table was covered with glass ashtrays, which we then put under the table. By some trick of the light, they showed up more clearly in the event than the faces of the members. I continued smoking my pipe, rather covertly, even within the DHSS, and I recall another occasion, soon after Sir George Godber — not a smoking man — had retired from the post of chief medical officer, and gone to live in Cambridge (in Almoner's Avenue, of all places). I was smoking quietly in my room when George, who was revisiting the department, looked in on me. To cover my confusion I said, "I always knew you could smell my pipe from the floor below, but I hadn't thought you could smell it from Cambridge." My ultimate — and I mean ultimate — cure came when I had gone to the Royal College of Physicians, and I owe it to the patient solicitation of my wife, and to the symbolic gesture of the registrar, David Pyke, who would respond to the lighting of a pipe by flinging open a window, even on the coldest day.

Over the past 50 years the preventive approach, so far from being neglected, has been intensively cultivated. A great deal of the credit for this has to go to general social improvements; to advances in the base of medical knowledge which contributed to prevention as well as to treatment; and to increased public awareness of health issues, and the part which individuals can play in preserving their own health. But the NHS has also played its part by making it easier for family doctors to see that the children are comprehensively immunised; by providing advice on health at all levels by doctors, nurses, and other health workers; and not least by timely interventions which prevent acute conditions from leading to chronic disability — an activity which can be variously called treatment or secondary prevention, depending on the point of view.

I hope I may have established that the NHS is good both for patients and for those in health who are liable to become patients — which means all of us. I believe it has also been good for doctors, by enabling them to practise medicine without having continually to be thinking, "Can this patient afford it?" (The more general question, "Can the country afford it?" I leave till later.) I do not think that my enthusiasm for the NHS has made me claim too much, as did the paediatric surgeon, anxious to demonstrate the breadth of his interests, who when asked to define the limits of his skills said, "I'll operate on any child" — and then added, as an afterthought, "or on anyone who has been a child."

A NATIONAL COMPARISON

As I am about to make a comparison which is not entirely favourable to medical care in the United States, I ought to make it clear that I do so from a base of strong friendship — for America in general, and more particularly for the many splendid American doctors whom I have met and known. But what I now have to say may be partly in reaction against the general (not universal) tendency of American writers on the NHS to see it as "socialised medicine," and to denigrate the standard of care which it provides.

It sometimes happens that a single conversation etches a concept in one's mind more effectively than all the reading in the world. I first visited the United States in 1956, and over a highball in Baltimore a Southern lady asked me, "Have you-all gotten penicillin in your health service?" I took some pleasure in explaining that we-all had, and indeed that penicillin was one of those British discoveries which we had left to the Americans to develop — at that time we were still in fact paying royalties on it. (Even the German annexation of "unser Shakespeare" had not carried a price tag.) On the same visit I heard on ward rounds discussion on whether this particular patient could afford the treatment — something that I had not heard at home for nearly a decade.

I would, of course, admit that it might have been better

for the present state of the NHS if we had given more thought earlier to the economic aspects. But is it such a bad bargain, in economic terms? We spend less than 7% of our national income on health care, while in the USA they spend over 10% of their larger per caput national income. Two important questions flow from this: Is the NHS highly economic, or is it under resourced? and, Is health care in the USA better or worse than in the UK? Paradoxically, the answer to each of these questions is, I believe, Both.

The NHS is certainly cheaper than the system of health care in the United States, and is thus comparatively economic, given that there is no great disparity of standards. But it is almost certainly under resourced, even though more money is being spent on it in this country than was the case 10 years ago. Like the red queen in *Through the Looking Glass*, we have to run faster just to stay where we are. Demography is against us, and medical advances, welcome though they are, scarcely lead to savings even if they are used, as they should be, with discrimination.

Because it costs more, is health care in the United States necessarily better than here? Fortunately for us, not so. As I have hinted, it is both better and worse — rather like private practice here, not surprisingly. Some things can be done in the USA to the highest standard, and for a higher proportion of those who need them, provided that they can also afford them. But at the other extreme, a destitute individual there cannot expect the care to which he is entitled here, and more generally there are areas in the USA whose public health services are rudimentary. There are also many places in the USA where general practice has virtually disappeared, though in other places attempts to revive it under the name of "primary care" are being made. I have already given my reasons for supposing that direct access to specialists is not a boon — and if there are no general practitioners, that is all a patient can seek. Doctors in the USA are wealthier than in the UK, but do not seem to be more loved.

I hope that having once made our escape in this country from a system of free enterprise in health we shall not

44

return to it. I am really quite optimistic that we shall not. After all, a system which has survived the financial strains and the triple reorganisation of the past 10 years must have considerable inherent strength and popular support. As a doctor, my testimony may be suspect, so let me end with a quotation from the sociologist, Rudolf Klein. Having noted current competitive and inegalitarian trends, he goes on to say, "To use the stonework of the NHS as the building material for a new society is to risk breaking up what remains, with all its imperfections, a formidable monument of social imagination without any certainty that the new structure will ever get beyond the planning stage of rhetoric."

4 A quiet grove?

Although the word "academic" is still applied to them, sometimes by way of criticism, our universities have moved some way from the olive grove of Academe in which Plato and Aristotle debated the great unsolved questions. The universal lust for cost effectiveness — "the price of everything and the value of nothing" — has affected them severely, for all their inherent strength and adaptability. The burden of straitened finances has fallen particularly heavily on the humanities, which are one half of the basis for distinguishing a university from a technical college. The other half is the study of the sciences, including medicine, in a way that brings out their theoretical basis as well as their application. I believe that a modern liberal education must include both of these elements, the arts and the sciences; and it is a matter of some regret that those who control our political destinies are so often careless, sometimes even proud, that they are ignorant of even the rudiments of science, however much they depend on it in daily living. As a general principle, and without relation to any particular example, it may be no bad thing that for the first time we have had as first minister of the crown a woman who had also had a training in science at first degree level. Nevertheless, the sciences also have been hit by a short sighted emphasis on the applied at the expense of the pure — as if these terms could be rigidly defined.

This mood has embarrassed both the universities and the research councils — the dual support system of research, of which this country had every reason to be proud, and which has been imitated in other countries and continents. I remember a meeting of the advisory board of the research councils some years ago, in which dutiful civil servants were promoting the view that money for research should be concentrated on underpinning those areas of manufacture that showed the greatest promise of expansion. The budget of the Science Research Council had just suffered a heavy cut, and the chairman, Sir Sam Edwards, exclaimed with a touch of *sang chaud*, "In that case, we should do more research on how to print banknotes."

I do not propose at this point to dwell on these present discontents. As an emeritus professor, I can only be a coat holder for those who are struggling against them; but I will later on say something of my personal involvement, in the mid-'seventies, with what has become known, perhaps unfairly, as the Rothschild debate on the control of publicly funded research. In the meantime, let me indulge myself in sincere praise and gratitude for institutions which have sustained me, materially and intellectually, ever since I matriculated at the University of St Andrews in 1930, apart from a year in hospital residence, and a few years of army service.

Although I learnt later on to appreciate the advantages of a large university in a large city, I think I was fortunate that my first three years of university life were spent in a small university in a country town. In those days the population of St Andrews was about 10 000. In term time this was increased by about 500 students, who stood out by virtue of their scarlet gowns, which gave some protection against the east wind that seemed more prevalent than the charts would suggest. In summer the students were replaced by golfers; but it was understood that the university was older than any of the four courses, which were free to townsfolk, and which were open to students for a fee of 10 shillings a year. Although a round of golf is a more or less pleasant way of taking a five mile walk, I discarded the clubs when I migrated to Oxford on a £200 a year research scholarship and discovered what a single round would cost.

Although Boswell in 1773 was dispirited "to see this ancient archiepiscopal seat now sadly deserted," and Samuel

Johnson's recorded conversation with the faculty was not inspiring, both town and gown have looked up since then. To live in a small town by the sea and to teach small classes are not undesirable things for a university professor, and they had certainly attracted scholars of eminence. The most distinguished of those whom I encountered, both in appearance with a white flowing beard, and in breadth of comprehension with equal competence in mathematics, Greek, and natural history, was D'Arcy Wentworth Thomson, a name to conjure with. In the zoology course of three terms, he talked to us for a term about a creature which he called "the little amoeba"; in the second term we progressed to the hydra. I now realise that he was teaching us general physiology, but for a narrow minded undergraduate surveying examination papers which included worms, fish, and even mammals, there was something of alarm in the slowness of the progression.

For an undergraduate, too, it was a great thing to be in a small company, mixing with students from other faculties, and hearing about their classes and their teachers, with no lack of emphasis on their eccentricities. These may be par for the course for professors of philosophy, but I think we had a real winner in Frederick Stout. Some professors in the arts faculty gave lectures both in St Andrews and Dundee; in those pre-Beeching days, St Andrews still had a railway station, but the journey to Dundee entailed changing trains at Leuchars junction. On one occasion Mrs Stout saw her husband on to the train, having furnished him with a ticket. Alas, he only got as far as Leuchars when confusion set in, but he had the presence of mind to get off the train and telephone his wife, to ask where he was going. With a touch of impatience, no doubt the product of similar problems in the past, she said, "Don't be silly, Freddie — look at your ticket." He did so, and returned to St Andrews. (I should point out that this allegation goes back to my student days, well before the currency of G K Chesterton's difficulty at Market Harborough.)

The clinical years in Dundee were rather less of an idyll, and the daily walk from Queen's College (now the separated

University of Dundee) to the infirmary, through the jute mills and marmalade factories, was not scenic, even though it lay between Dundee Law and the Firth of Tay, with the stumps of the first railway bridge whose collapse is described in *Hatter's Castle*. There were too many lectures, and on the whole they were rather dull — though I expect that by now I must have transmitted to Manchester students as much boredom as I sustained in Dundee.

Although a research fellow works in a university department, and may teach students, he is not really a member of the university staff. Moreover, if the department in which he works is a clinical one, centred in the hospital, he may see very little of the university life around him, especially if he is not working in his own alma mater. It is no reflection on the kindness of the people with whom I worked if I say that my five years in Oxford and Cambridge gave me little insight into the inner life of these places, or into the complex relationship between the colleges and the university in either place. I have, however, been told that an outsider can spend a lifetime in either place without attaining any greater understanding than I did. The Duke of Wellington had two rules of public speaking: "I never speak of what I know nothing, and I never quote Latin." So let me obey at any rate the first of these rules, and hurry on to my first "proper" post on the staff of a university. As I outlined in my first chapter, this came in 1946, on my discharge from the army, and was that of a lecturer in the department of medicine in Manchester. I have already said something of my clinical work there, but I now want to say something of the university of which I have been a member for 40 years.

Already one of the larger civic universities when I first knew it, Manchester has more than doubled in size since then, with a far sighted cooperation between the university and the civic authorities which has allowed the development of a campus extending from the hospitals and parent university at the south end to the University of Manchester Institute of Science and Technology at the other. The citizens of Manchester are justly proud of their university, and of its history — when I was there, bus conductors still called out "Owen's College," and the title, Victoria University of Manchester, is still used, although the organic links with other northern universities have gone. Prominent citizens were happy to serve on the council, and ultimately to chair it; and their contribution was vital in achieving a balance between financial solvency in hard times and the pursuit of academic excellence, to which they were equally devoted. For many years the responsibility for the financial side of things lay with R A Rainford, who must have been the outstanding bursar of his generation (although as a young Turk of a lecturer I had suggested he should be given the title of professor of false economy, I came to appreciate fully the difficulty of his task in meeting conflicting claims, and the skill with which he discharged it — and indeed I am still appreciating his work, for he was one of the founding fathers of the university superannuation scheme, from which I draw my academic pension; I shudder to think what kind of mess I would have made of the previous financial arrangements on retirement).

When I first went to Manchester the vice chancellor was Sir John Stopford, or to give him the full name which his parents chose for him, John Sebastian Bach Stopford — a choice which ensured that with all his outstanding abilities only one was lacking: appreciation of music. An anatomist of distinction who had collaborated with Telford, the surgeon, in early studies of the sympathetic nervous system, he contrived somehow to give total and devoted service to his own university which he loved; to be a national leader in the university world; and to be the first chairman of the regional hospital board when it was set up. He was also an elder of the Fallowfield Presbyterian church. Those were the days in which a vice chancellor was allowed, perhaps even expected, to be something of a dictator, provided he was benevolent, and above all fair. As a junior lecturer I did not hobnob with vice chancellors, but he knew all his staff, and occasionally had the disconcerting habit of asking us to see some ailing colleague in another faculty — it was in that context that I learnt the importance of including the general practitioner in any such transaction.

In due course Stopford was succeeded by the registrar of the university, the distinguished lawyer who was to become Sir William Mansfield Cooper, and also of course a leading vice chancellor nationally and internationally. I have already mentioned his kindness in coming to tell me personally of my appointment to the chair of medicine; what I should now say is that this was typical of the man — he resembled John Stopford not only in subtlety of thought and plainness of speech, but also in having the common touch both in public address and in private conversation. What was perhaps different between the two men was the climate in which they worked. Cooper was certainly no more dirigiste than Stopford, perhaps even less so; but the constraints on leadership became much greater in the 'fifties and 'sixties. Universities became much larger, and to that extent less controllable ; power sharing and democratisation found champions both in the sciences and in the social sciences; and there was a high tide of student demonstrations and sit-ins. Although it was not in his nature to complain, I felt great sympathy for my vice chancellor when he could no longer rely fully on the support of all his colleagues in resisting actions that disrupted the proper function of a university. (Having implied the heresy of being a conservative in university affairs, may I compound it by expressing the view that the Robbins policy of unrestricted entry to the university system may have had unfortunate consequences, in lessening the appreciation among students that they were in any way privileged by having been admitted to university studies.)

For the last decade or so of my time in Manchester Sir Arthur Armitage was vice chancellor. Also a lawyer, he came back to his native Lancashire from what — to an outsider at least — seems an idyllic post, that of president of Queens' College, Cambridge. Although he had not the oratorical gifts of his two predecessors, he was their equal in penetration and in strength of character. By the time he took over I had become more senior in the university, and of course we were more nearly equal in age; so we became firm friends, and in the last year of my stay in Manchester

I was one of his four pro-vice chancellors. I can recall only one occasion on which we disagreed. I had become chairman of one of the university's halls of residence, Needham Hall, and the warden called me in because of a student who persistently refused to wear a tie for the evening meal, having signed a declaration at the beginning of term that he would abide by a number of provisions, including the one about ties. Importantly, it was a complaint by the other students which decided the warden that the defaulting student should be asked either to comply or to seek other accommodation. I saw the student together with the warden, and emphasised that, while wearing a tie was a triviality, departing from a signed undertaking was not. When I discussed this later with Arthur Armitage he thought we should have overlooked the matter — he may have been right, and for a few days I had visions of headlines in the press, "Student dismissed from hall for not wearing a tie." But my luck held, the student left the hall, and Fleet Street remained untroubled by this storm in a northern teacup. I have mentioned that single divergence of view, but in all else we were in sympathy and I was very sad that Arthur was able to enjoy no more than a short period of retirement.

When I look back on what must be accounted a successful career, and seek for reasons why this may have been so, one factor must surely have been my good fortune in never becoming dean of a medical school; by the time I reached an appropriate level of seniority I was already cocooned in protective national commitments. But I have been the grateful beneficiary of other occupants of such offices. The first dean with whom I became associated with was H S Raper, an authority on lipid metabolism in the days when it was a respectable academic study and not the plaything of nutritional lobbies and commercial interests. When he retired from the chair of physiology he was made a full time dean; and in due course I became what was called tutor in the faculty of medicine. This meant assisting the dean at meetings, and also sitting in with him at interviews of prospective students. The romantic side of his nature was mainly expressed in exquisite watercolours of Yorkshire scenes. He was less impressed by students who paraded, say, their presidency in school debating societies, for he would ask them, "Did you settle anything?" The next dean was Walter Schlapp, professor of physiology, who made up for any deficiencies in Stopford's musical abilities by playing the viola in the same quartet in which Eric Ashby played a violin and Robert Platt the cello.

Fond as I was of both Raper and Schlapp, I may sometimes have disappointed them by my pragmatic attitude to academic propriety, for I have always believed, with Max Rosenheim, that one should "play the rules according to the game," rather than the other way round. In that respect at least, I was more at home with my next two deans, J H Kellgren and Colin Campbell. Jonky Kellgren was one of the leaders in establishing the study of the diseases of joints as the academic and clinical specialty of rheumatology; he was also particularly clear sighted in bringing scientific rigour, including allowance for observer error, into the delineation of the rheumatic diseases at both the individual and the population level. Colin Campbell, who succeeded him as dean, was professor of pathology, whose knowledge and enthusiasm made him one of the best teachers in the school. By their influence in the university, and ultimately by their advocacy to the University Grants Committee, these two men secured the building of the new medical school, the Stopford Building, which replaces the Victorian edifice that was opened by T H Huxley.

Every rose has its thorn; and the new medical school, which was certainly badly needed, was won only at the expense of an expansion of medical student entry from around 100 to well over 200, with a further expansion in the clinical years due to the admission of students who had done their preclinical work in St Andrews. Medical student numbers are a bit like jam in heaven — they may have been right in the past, and may again be right in the future, but they are never right in the present. The Willink committee underestimated the need for doctors in the 'fifties; but in the late 'sixties this had probably been over corrected in what was being planned for the future. Although it is in fact true, present day professors of medicine may find it hard to believe that at that time I was asked more than once by the dean whether I could accommodate another lecturer in medicine. Not perhaps the best way to run a university, but certainly no worse than the present method of unreflecting financial constraints and redundancies, which fall most heavily on faculties with a high turnover of staff — and this includes the medical faculty because of interchanges of clinical staff with the NHS.

As a St Andrews graduate I have occasionally been taxed with or praised for the decision to accommodate the St Andrews students in the clinical years. Given the clinical facilities in the hospitals of the north west region, I certainly agreed with the decision; but the initiative lay with the deans, and particularly with the executive dean, Bill Beswick, who felt that the quality of entrants to the clinical years might be safeguarded if we had another catchment area.

The expansion of university accommodation had of course to be matched by increased clinical facilities for teaching. In addition to the Royal Infirmary, adjacent to the university, Withington Hospital has been developed as the University Hospital of South Manchester, and Hope Hospital in Salford as a third teaching hospital. Moreover, students in their second clinical year, normally the fifth year of their course, are attached for months on end to district hospitals in the region. This was a controversial decision at the time, but I believe it has worked out well and I strongly supported it, in the belief that students really learn from experience of patients, under ordinary competent supervision, rather than from completely centralised teaching, which may even carry some risk of super specialisation, or of pyrotechnics by the more flamboyant professional teachers. And to look at it from the other side, it would scarcely be held that the staff of district hospitals would not benefit from having students attached to them.

One of the things that protect a professor of medicine from the danger of enjoying life too much is his certain membership of a curriculum committee, which in turn is likely to be a standing committee of the faculty. Certainly

Aged 12 at South Kirriemuir

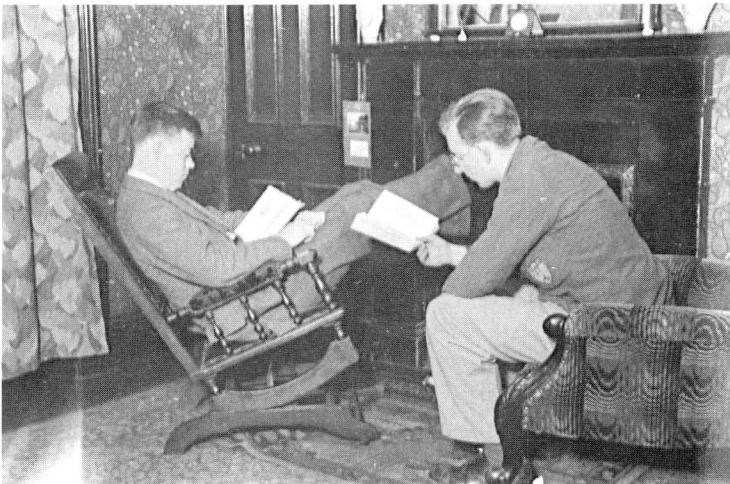

Black and White. With J R A White, fellow medical student at Dundee

RAMC

The spirit of research. Dr D A K Black, Oxford 1939 (candid camera
by Dr Charles Fletcher)

Wedding day, 10 April 1948

With Dr Nigel Compston

Awake in a meeting

medicine changes rapidly enough, and the proper emphasis to be placed on its component parts varies enough, to justify keeping the curriculum under review. On the other hand, the division of a medical school into separate departments tends to make the synoptic view take second place to the determination of each department to give nothing away. To rise above the grinding of axes, advocacy of the long term interests of the students has to be persistent, sometimes even strident. Then again, there is the consoling thought that widely different curricula seem to produce remarkably similar products, and almost certainly the most important determinant of what comes out is in fact what goes in, the intervening process being important, it is true, but less important than a good quality of entrant. For this reason, I commend the practice in Manchester of having prospective entrants talk to current students, so that they have at least a chance of assessing whether the course is likely to suit them — a disappointed student is not likely to be a good student.

Manchester University was one of the first in this country to develop a centre for general practice, originally in Darbishire House Health Centre. Stopford and Robert Platt were the chief initiators and early supporters of the scheme, but in due course it fell to me to chair the Darbishire House committee, which gave me the great joy of working with the first professor of general practice in the university, Pat Byrne, who later became president of the Royal College of General Practitioners. Described by one of his referees as "an Irishman of great charm" (almost a tautology), Pat effected a synthesis of educational techniques and practical experience which has had great influence on the present day training for general practice. A university connection did not always ensure a warm benediction from established local practitioners. I was the university representative on the local committee regulating the appointment of trainers in general practice — an appointment which carried an emolument for the trainer. When an application came from one of the doctors in Darbishire House to be a trainer, another member of the committee suggested that since he was already teaching undergraduates, it would not be fair that he should be training graduates as well. It was left to me to point out that an exclusion on these lines would equally debar almost all university teachers, including myself.

In the days when there was money for new initiatives, these were planned by the development committee, and then submitted to the senate and council. As a member of that committee, and also of the standing committee of senate, which carried out a massive exercise annually on the promotion of staff, I became, if not involved, at any rate acquainted with the problems of other faculties and with the tension between research achievement and teaching ability as a ground for promotion. I was also, of course, a member of search committees for occupants of chairs in the medical faculty, once I had myself been appointed a professor. (While one is still seeking a chair, the universe seems encumbered with brilliant young coevals, and one finds oneself "desiring this man's art and that man's scope." But when one has been appointed to a chair, the scene changes overnight, the galaxy of talent disappears, and mediocrity appears to take sway.)

I greatly enjoyed these contacts with the wider university world, perhaps more friendly to members of another faculty than to closer colleagues. I remember Patrick Blackett explaining to Robert Platt that the reason progress in medicine was so slow, compared with particle physics, was not that doctors were stupid, but that the problems themselves were so much more difficult. I remember the excitement when Bernard Lovell at last got the money for Jodrell Bank — including a contribution from members of staff. I perhaps could claim to own a rivet of that mighty structure. We had a liaison with the University of Strasbourg, and I was going into lunch with Eugene Vinaver when we passed a one volume book, *A Compendium of Universal Knowledge*, and I elicited a Gallic smile by pointing out how small it seemed. And, of course, Freddie Williams was building the first working computer, with valves instead of chips.

Back to medicine. Just before my own final exam Adam

Patrick addressed us with the cheering word that he "would always give the benefit of the doubt," but added "to the general public." It is a solemn thing to loose on to the world someone who shows little sign of competence. On the other hand, the alternative is not very clearly obvious — someone who has spent five years, or quite possibly more, in the pursuit of a qualification is not likely to be thwarted in the long run. And I have never had much faith in the magical effect of six months' referral, though a good short term result can in fact be achieved by intensive coaching. (This was shown in an experiment carried out by Robert Platt — half a dozen "chronic" failures were collected in the medical unit, and grilled intensively in the basics of clinical medicine for six months, at the end of which time five of them passed — sorry, no follow up available.)

On the whole, the plan that I adopted was to be as liberal as possible in letting people through, trying hard to overcome the suspicion with which the teetering student regards anyone who is trying to steer him towards the right answer. Even so, a hard core of frankly dangerous people remains, though a much smaller one than is often supposed; very often the trouble was psychological rather than purely intellectual, and counselling was needed in addition to referral. I was also very reluctant to fail anyone on the quality of their essay writing, and I had an argument with George Pickering over this. We were agreed that it would be a good thing if doctors could write well and clearly; but since most of a doctor's communication is verbal or even non-verbal rather than in the essay form, I could not see this as a hanging matter. A further consideration is that, in contrast to the way it was in my own student days, the medical graduate is not loosed straightway into independent practice. Passing the final exam is only "the end of the beginning"; and some years of supervised training lie ahead, very likely entailing further examination on specialised subjects.

Just as the purpose of appointments committees is to bring out the qualities of the candidates and not the brilliance of committee members, so the purpose of examinations is to test the competence of the student and not the cleverness of the examiner. I learnt this lesson rather early, in the (to me) memorable setting of my own final exam in medicine. Even in those days, the device for draining fluid from the tissues known as Southey's tubes was scarcely a matter of daily use, and it is now a museum piece. I was given the constituents of what I think an engineer would call a "blown up" Southey's tube, and asked to fit them together. I did so, and handed them back to the external examiner, the paediatrician Leonard Finlay, who had not yet migrated from Glasgow to Shadwell. With the ghost of a smile he dived into his trouser pocket, opened his hand, and said, "What about this wee screw?" A few years later, during the war, I found myself in the same lodgings in Oxford as Leonard Finlay, and got to know him and like him, but at that time the appreciation of the joke was distinctly unilateral.

A valuable check on the fairness, quality, and general uniformity of the qualifying examinations is given by the system of external examiners. Anyone who wants to talk to a professor of medicine in the second half of June must be prepared to travel, but the interchange is a valuable one, not only in the context of the examinations. Mostly, appointment as an examiner is for a three year stint, so over the years I was able to examine in six medical schools in England, two in Scotland, and three in Ireland. In Belfast, John Vallance-Owen inherited me from Graham Bull, who had left for Northwick Park; and I remember the high quality of students in the province, as well as lunchtime strolls in the Falls Road nearby — *eheu fugaces*. In Cambridge, with its small hinterland and large body of students, mostly at that time trained in the London hospitals, even the external examiner got to know some of the patients rather well, especially those from John Walshe's flock of patients with Wilson's disease — I suspect the students also knew them. Most of the internal examiners in London were part time, so the oral exams took place only in the afternoon, giving the provincial examiner a bonus of free mornings and evenings in London. In other places the burden of examining (and it is in fact a stressful occupation for the examiner, though students will never believe this) is relieved by pleasant hospitality in the evenings — in Manchester we took our team out to Disley to play very amateur bowls on a midge infested crown green.

External examining is not the only outside commitment that is likely to come the way of a professor of medicine. Others include conferences at home and abroad; membership of national bodies; and an occasional lecture tour abroad for a longer period. I was fortunate enough to have one such tour as a Sims professor to Australia and New Zealand, with stops in Singapore on the way out and Kuala Lumpur on the way back. This was in 1971, and not only did we leave England on the day decimal currency came in — so I have never quite caught up — but it was also the year of the long postal strike, so that it became something of an adventure trip. Programmes sent in advance had not arrived, so on reaching each centre the first inquiry had to be, "When do I give the first talk?" These tours teach you the meaning of full employment, and it is a tremendous help on a long tour to be sustained by a wife who can bear the conversational brunt in the evening. Always carry slides in your hand luggage — Max Rosenheim lost his in Karachi on the way out, and some weeks later was reported as getting on the return plane at Perth muttering hoarsely, "Please, not another patient with hypertension and renal failure."

I represented my university on the General Medical Council for a few years in the 'sixties, when Henry Cohen in his second five year term was still displaying all the arts of a directionist chairman in keeping democracy at bay. Appearances were deceptive: he was one of the kindest of men, as I learnt from what I am happy to say was my only experience of being on the disciplinary subcommittee. In the days before David Steel's Abortion Act we had an extensive illegal import trade in abortees from the Continent; a taxi driver had a pack of a certain doctor's visiting cards, and alleged that he had been given them by the doctor, so that he could bring ladies to his surgery. The doctor's story was that he had lost the cards, and the taxi driver must have found them. I formed a view on the relative credibility of these two stories; but in his direction to us Henry Cohen stressed the lack of corroboration of either story, and the doctor remained on the register.

My most congenial and absorbing external commitment, however, followed my appointment to the Medical Research Council as an independent scientific member in 1966. I took the place of Max Rosenheim, at the end of his four year period of membership, and joined Melville Arnott as the other physician on the council. The chairman of council was Lord Amory, who as Heathcoat Amory had been Chancellor of the Exchequer; and the secretary, who is of course not a clerk but the senior executive and accounting officer of council, was Sir Harold Himsworth. Much of the detailed work of the council was done by the clinical research board (CRB) and the biological research board (BRB); as a clinician, I was naturally on the clinical research board, which at that time was chaired by Robert Platt. In general terms, the boards dealt with visits to the council's units and other establishments, and also to recipients of long term grants in the universities and with the assessment of major applications for research money, the smaller applications being dealt with by grants committees. The council determined the allocation of money to the two boards, and also determined matters of general policy, which included the assessment of the relative priority of broad areas of research; the balance between training grants and the support of established workers; and the very important balance between direct support of research in the council's own establishments and indirect support of research carried out in university departments. At that time direct and indirect support, as just defined, were roughly equal, and the term dual support system was justified. As times have become harder, both for councils and universities, I understand that the balance has moved a little way towards direct support, as the council's first general priority must be to maintain that for which it is directly responsible. This is not the place to attempt a general history of the council, which has in any case been admirably told by Sir Arthur Landsborough Thomson.

Although the council met only once a month, other than August, the work entailed in visits, in meetings of the board, and in assessment of papers must have averaged one day a week. Almost all of it was enjoyable, and a particular feature was the lunchtime sessions, at which experts gave informal accounts of their work, followed by discussion. Perhaps I can illustrate the quality of Amory's chairmanship by one recollection of such a meeting, addressed by the ethologist Niko Tinbergen. Among much else, he told us that if chaffinch eggs were incubated, the young birds would learn to sing only if taught by other chaffinches; and he added that they would learn more quickly and better from their parents than from other birds. Amory's comment on that was, "I wish pop singers were like that."

One of the council's methods of working was to set up committees to consider what could be done to develop specific topics of research. The members of such committees were of course mainly experts, but the chairman tended to be a generalist member of council. I chaired one such committee on biochemical aspects of psychiatry (being neither a biochemist nor a psychiatrist), and after a pretty faltering start through what was to me an uncharted minefield we did produce in the end a report which had some influence on policy. What it taught me was the patience to listen to various points of view, and to extract from them some kind of message which could be understood. I was destined to have some further practice of this peculiar art.

Three big issues arose during my first period on the MRC. Perhaps the largest of these, the control by the government of the research for which it supplied the money, I shall leave to the next chapter. The other two were the appointment of a successor to Harry Himsworth, and a review of the board structure of the MRC.

During the quite lengthy discussions in council on the first of these matters, my friend Alastair Currie and I were asked to leave, so it was fairly obvious that we were possible candidates. Good fortune consists not only in getting things but also in failing to get things, and I count myself extremely fortunate not to have got this particular appointment, for I would certainly have done it badly as I have no patience with figures, and little understanding of them, and my appetite for intricate arguments on either administration or scientific policy is rapidly saturated. Eventually the lot fell to John Gray, the then second secretary of council; he was infinitely better equipped than either Alastair or myself to thread the maze which was opening up before the council in the next five years. He had a splendid grasp of principle and infinite patience with detail, and I found it a joy to work with him, both in council and later when I was in the DHSS.

The details of board structure would interest only professional committee watchers. But the major transition was from so called vertical boards (the existing structure of CRB and BRB), to horizontal boards (the present structure of neurosciences board, cell board, and systems board). The reason for the change was to bring clinicians and more basic workers together within each of the new boards, instead of separating them into CRB and BRB. By the time a decision came to be reached, Lord Amory had been succeeded as chairman of council by the Duke of Northumberland (who came to us from the Agricultural Research Council, as Amory put it, "dripping with foot and mouth"); John Gray was secretary; and I had become chairman of the CRB. Together with Peter Walker, of Edinburgh, who was chairman of the BRB, we had many discussions and eventually decided to recommend this change to council. I am not sure that we got it right. We certainly complicated the board structure; and more speculatively, we may have prejudiced the funding of clinical research, which was in a way protected when it had a separate board, but which now had to face competition from colleagues on the same board whose problems lent themselves more easily to concrete expression.

In that last paragraph I have to some extent jumped ahead, as these discussions took place after I had left the council at the end of my period in 1970. I was sorry to go, but had the distraction of my Sims lecture visit to Australia to look forward to. I was called out from dinner one evening in Melbourne to take a telephone call; it was John Gray, asking if I would be chairman of the CRB in the coming year. I had no difficulty in agreeing subject to the consent of my vice chancellor, for not only had I greatly enjoyed my period on the council but I was proud to be the third Manchester chairman of the board, after Robert Platt. The first chairman of the board was our distinguished neuro-surgeon, Sir Geoffrey Jefferson, who understood everything except the passage of time.

5 Inside the Elephant (1973-7)

At birth each one of us is a potential Jack of all trades, but as we grow older we have to make choices between the various options, until finally we are committed by training and circumstances to a particular career. Along this road, each positive choice forfeits the opportunity of doing something else; in a way this is analogous to the "opportunity cost," the name economists use to denote the sacrifice of other opportunities which we make whenever we commit resources to a particular objective. As a teenager I had toyed with the prospect of becoming a civil servant — this was of course in the days when the civil service and even politics in this country were generally respected. As a young doctor I appreciated the value of changing the nature of one's job, and even the place where one did it, at intervals of a few years. As I mounted the academic ladder in Manchester I would have been greatly surprised to be told that as I approached the age of 60 I would again become occupationally mobile, and that the long forgotten option of being a civil servant would once again open before me. In this chapter I describe how this came about, and what I made of it.

When I succeeded Sir Brian Windeyer as chairman of the clinical research board in 1971 I became more closely concerned in the conduct of the Medical Research Council than I had been as an independent member in the late 'sixties. As a successor body to the Medical Research Committee set up during the first world war, the MRC was the oldest of the five research councils, the others being the Science Research Council, the Agricultural Research Council, the Natural Environment Research Council, and the Social Sciences Research Council. Although funded almost entirely by government money, the research councils rather jealously guarded their freedom from direct intervention by the various administrative departments of government — a state of affairs which derived sanction from the "Haldane principle," dating back to 1918, which advocated the administrative independence of a government research organisation from other departments of government. The council system, acting with scientific independence, had by no means been unproductive of practical benefits some of which, like cephalosporin, even attained the coveted distinction of commercial profitability. Freedom from administrative control does not necessarily rule out effective influence, and where there was a clear relationship between a research council and a service department, mechanisms were set up to allow this. In the particular case of the MRC and the health departments, the chief medical officers of the health departments attended council meetings as assessors, and could often pledge the help of the departments in joint projects involving the facilities of the NHS; moreover, the health departments nominated five of the 12 members of the clinical research board.

Nevertheless, and in spite of much successful cooperation, the value and validity of the scientific independence of the research councils was increasingly questioned. With more complex research methods and the growth of teamwork, research became more expensive; this strengthened the resolve of the piper to have more control over the choice of tune. More specifically, the health departments and the MRC quite reasonably attached different priorities to particular aspects of research, the departments looking mainly for practical utility, the MRC for scientific excellence and feasibility. Under the leadership of George Godber and of Dick Cohen (who went from the MRC to the DHSS with a view to setting up a research division within the department), considerable direct DHSS support was given to health service research, carried out usually independently of the MRC, but sometimes jointly as in the epidemiology and medical care unit at Northwick Park. Perhaps I am by nature inclined to complacency, but my general view at the time was that this dual system, whereby the MRC supported basic and clinical research, and the health departments supported health service research, was working rather well. But a considerable spanner was on its way into the works, in the shape of the Rothschild report.

This was a terse document of two dozen pages which dismissed the Haldane view in a sentence — "The concepts of scientific independence used in the Haldane Report are not relevant to contemporary discussion of Government research." Rothschild's substitute for scientific independence was the customer-contractor principle, again definable in a Rothschild sentence: "The customer says what he wants; the contractor does it (if he can); and the customer pays." As a paying customer obviously needs some money, and new money (as ever) was not to be found, the councils in varying degree suffered a transfer of funds, which they had previously enjoyed from the Department of Education and Science, to the customer departments; in the case of the MRC this amounted to a quarter of its previous budget, and the Agricultural Research Council (of which Rothschild had been previously chairman) was even harder hit, with a 50% transfer to the Ministry of Agriculture, Fisheries and Food (MAFF). The expectation was that the customer departments would give the corresponding council at any rate the opportunity to carry out research commissioned in this way. Of course, translation of departmental objectives, as seen by ministers or senior administrative civil servants into researchable projects is not an easy matter; the task of doing so was to be entrusted to a chief scientist in the customer department. He would be assisted by an organisation based on the research division of the department, and would work in close harmony with the administrative head of the relevant council, who would carry out the task allotted to Rothschild's controller of research and development — in other words be responsible for the completion of the contract.

These proposals were presented to parliament in a green paper in November 1971, together with a paper from Sir

Frederick Dainton which took a different view; but the anonymous memorandum by the government which preceded the green paper endorsed the customer-contractor principle, thereby giving a pretty clear indication of how things were going. Time was allowed for "wide public debate and to discuss the issues with the scientific community" — which meant until the end of February 1972, including a bonus day since that was a leap year. Not surprisingly, the reaction of scientists, and particularly of those working with the research councils, was critical. Max Perutz in *Nature* compiled an impressive roll of practical achievements stemming from research carried out by the MRC. Brian Windeyer and I wrote a joint letter to *The Times* (11 January 1972), in which we tried to correct Rothschild's impression of "the rather small size of the DHSS and SHHD [Scottish Home and Health Department] participation in the MRC's affairs." Perhaps the most forthright criticism appeared in *The Times* the same day from Lord Halsbury:

Nothing in this world is perfect. Everything benefits from criticism. If the DHSS or MAFF are critical of the programmes authorized by the MRC and the ARC the proper place for their comments to be voiced is at CSP [Council for Scientific Policy] level. The machinery is there. Our task is to use it effectively. Instead we are tinkering with the works while indulging our national passion for collective nagging, thereby eroding our morale in the hope of restoring our steadily declining fortunes.

In July 1972 the government published its white paper, *Framework for Government Research and Development*, which broadly accepted the Rothschild proposals. Shortly after, I made the interesting discovery that even if you are not on the winning side in a policy discussion, to have been on the losing side with reasoned argument does not protect you from being asked to help in the new set up. George Godber and John Gray asked me to consider taking the post of chief scientist in the DHSS, and I agreed, after a day or two of painful reflection that it meant leaving clinical work, leaving Manchester, and learning to operate a system about which I had some misgivings. I was, however, glad to learn that Drew Kay (professor of surgery in Glasgow, now Sir Andrew Kay) had agreed to be chief scientist at the Scottish Home and Health Department.

Before giving my general impressions of life in a large government department, let me carry through my account of the roles of the DHSS and the MRC in sponsoring research to the time when I lost touch with the problem. Dick Cohen became the first DHSS chief scientist for six months while I was loosening my ties with Manchester, and learning the ropes in the department. The research division of the department was in the administrative charge of an under secretary, who at that time was Ken Stowe, destined later to become permanent secretary of the DHSS, an advancement which may support my belief that he is one of the most effective people with whom I have ever worked. In 1972 it was still possible to believe that research was a growth industry, and that resources would be found even for administering it, let alone actually doing it. So these two embarked with a will on setting up an administrative structure that would do justice to the vision of the Rothschild report, now incarnated as government policy. Part time scientists from outside the department were brought in to constitute a "chief scientist's committee," which included doctors, nurses, economists, sociologists, social administrators and so on. There were subordinate committees to deal with health service research, personal social services research, and research related to social security. For the specific task of commissioning research from the MRC, a panel on medical research was set up. In order to flesh out the customer-contractor concept, a system of research liaison groups (RLGs) was inaugurated.

I should explain that the wide ranging responsibilities of the DHSS are divided among some 15 to 20 divisions, each headed by an under secretary, who was nominated as the "customer." It was his job, with appropriate advice, to lay down priorities; and to help in this he had his professional colleagues within his division, outside experts in the appropriate area, and people from the research management division to do the actual commissioning of research, once agreed. These things all more or less flowed from a sincere attempt to implement the customer-contractor principle. But before I leave this picture of the projected administration, I must mention the one component of the new administration which was alien to the customer-contractor principle, and which by one of fate's little ironies is almost the sole surviving part of what we set up. (I say "we" because of course I was concerned in all this from the start, and was directly responsible for persuading outside scientists to come in and help the department in these various ways.) The discrepant mechanism to which I have just referred is the small grants committee, which recognised that if people were to be encouraged to take up research related to the provision of services, they must be able to enjoy modest support at a stage before their reputation was so high as to commend them to a generalist under secretary; so we committed a comparatively modest sum of money to the heretical enormity of actually asking scientists to put forward proposals for doing what they actually wanted to do, as opposed to obeying the behest of a customer.

When I took over in April 1973 the main committees had already been formed, but only a start had been made on the RLG system. The original intention was to extend this system (which after all was the purest example of the customer-contractor principle in action) to all the divisions of the DHSS; but in fact it never got more than half way, for two main reasons. The first of these was the progressive limitation of resources which set in, diminishing both the total research budget, and more specifically the budget for research administration, including cuts in the staff available to work the new system. The second reason was the varying attitudes of the divisional under secretaries to their new responsibilities as "customers." It was rare indeed for any of them to welcome the new role with open arms — some were lukewarm from the beginning, others were soon diverted by more pressing preoccupations. The initial enthusiasm of outside advisers soon cooled, though there were honourable exceptions where an RLG actually worked, notably the RLG for the nursing division. The chief scientist's committee worked well for the time that I knew it, but has since fallen a victim to cuts; similarly with the personal social services research group. The health services research board is a sadder tale. Reasonably enough, it was made a national body for the United Kingdom; but this automatically made it too large, for health service research is of its nature multidisciplinary. Since every disciplinary Englishman had to be matched by a correspondingly disciplinary Scot, and since the exchange of views between disciplines is commendable in theory but difficult in practice, the board never gelled in the way that the chief scientist's committee did.

For somewhat different reasons, the panel on medical research was also a failure, and was disbanded in due course. The root cause of failure was the inability of anyone in the department, including myself, to conjure up specific commissions for the MRC which would even remotely match the £5 million of transferred funds. A somewhat shallow respectability was provided by the device of broad commissions which we evolved in concert with John Gray and his colleagues at the MRC, and to which we were in effect driven by the failure of Rothschild and those who followed him to realise that clinical research was of the highest importance to the department in general, but was not readily segmented into specific commissions. This arrangement led to a zareba of triple accountancy, in which each head of commissioned expenditure had to be accounted for once as departmental expenditure by the permanent secretary, DHSS; and twice by the secretary of the MRC — once as part of the transferred funds, and again as part of the total MRC budget. This system also provoked acid comments from the directors of MRC units, chosen for research ability rather than for accounting skills, when they were asked to divide their accounts between "transferred funds" and "direct council support." Looking ahead, it came as a considerable relief when towards the end of my time in the DHSS Jim Gowans was able to persuade Pat Nairne that scientists might in fact be quite good judges of what was worth doing, and what was feasible, and would be more profitably employed in research than in splitting their unit expenditure between transferred funds and direct MRC funding.

Without denying that there is a place for commissioned research where the end product can be clearly specified, my experience in the DHSS convinced me that commissioning has little relevance to the type of research which is useful in relation to the responsibility of the DHSS, and certainly not to clinical research. The really important long term benefits in medicine come not from mission oriented research (what Bacon called *experimenta fructifera*), but from research which illuminates important general problems (Bacon's *experimenta lucifera*). I have indicated that I held a similar view before entering the DHSS, so I suspect that I may be vulnerable to criticism of two kinds. Holding such views, should I have agreed to enter the DHSS? And did I really try to make the system work? My own answer, at the conscious level, is Yes to both these questions. And I guess the same holds good for my successors Arthur Buller and Desmond Pond, and now for Francis O'Grady.

After a confession that the main purpose of my entering the DHSS fell far short of realisation, it may come as something of a surprise when I say that I both enjoyed and profited from the few years I spent there. Soon after I left the DHSS for the Royal College of Physicians I sat next to David Ennals at dinner, and with something less than his usual tact he asked me if I had enjoyed working in his department. I answered, truthfully, that I had made a point of enjoying every post that I had held; and I left it to him to interpret my rider that some were more difficult to enjoy than others.

My enjoyment came very largely from the quality of the people with whom I found myself working, both those within the department, and those whom I recruited from "the field," as the outside world was termed. I was, of course, already familiar with that part of "the field" which was medical, but my two biggest surprises on entering the department were that the health service formed quite a small part of the total interests of the DHSS, which included also the personal social services, and beyond that the mammoth operation of social security; and, further, that the health service, which from the outside seemed so integrally connected with the DHSS, was commonly looked on from the inside as something very much external to the department, and rather troublesome at that.

As used in the civil service, permanent is a relative term, applied to the highest grade, the administrative heads and accounting officers of a department. During only four years, I served with two permanent secretaries, and two chief medical officers (who hold permanent rank). Perhaps the permanence is in comparison with secretaries of state, of whom I had three — Keith Joseph, Barbara Castle, and David Ennals — as well as a kaleidoscope of junior ministers, including at different times David Owen, Roland Moyle, and Alfred Morris.

To start with the politicians, I had comparatively little to do with them directly, for research is neither a vote catcher nor a vote loser, and though the money spent on it by the DHSS was not negligible, it was of course small change compared with what was spent on the health service, which in turn was dwarfed by the spending on social security — pensions, sickness benefits, supplementary benefits, and so on. On the other hand, since the official duty of a departmental civil servant is to support his political masters of the day by all honourable means, and since I was within the charmed circle at a fairly senior level, I did hear a good deal of what went on, particularly by attending the regular meetings held both by the permanent secretary and the chief medical officer, at which policy was discussed and the wishes of ministers were revealed by implication, if not directly. There were also occasional meetings with ministers when some political issue had a research aspect, including the possibility of postponing a troublesome decision "pending the result of further research."

At Secretary of State level, I can only remember two occasions on which a positive and informed stimulus was given to research, and happily for my neutrality they came from opposite sides of the political divide. The first of these was Keith Joseph's sponsorship of research into "the cycle of transmitted deprivation," — that is, the tendency for adverse social circumstances to afflict the children and even the grandchildren of deprived parents. He may have coined this phrase himself, and research was commissioned on a considerable scale from the Social Science Research Council, without so far as I know anyone spoiling a good problem by solving it. I think there may always have been a tension between genuine social compassion and orthodox monetarism in Keith Joseph's mind; and I am sure that political expediency ranked well below either. Another Secretary of State who actually wanted to do good was David Ennals; and his compassion, while wide ranging, became to some extent focused on the well recognised disadvantage of lower paid manual workers, in terms of ill health and premature death, by comparison with the wealthier sections of the population. He asked me to convene a working group to assemble information on inequalities in health related to social class; to unearth possible causal relationships between poverty and ill health; and to consider implications for policy. When I agreed to do this, early in 1977, I did not know that within a month or two I would be leaving the DHSS, still less that our report would take three years to prepare. But both these stories come later on.

Not surprisingly, the minister who took the most direct and informed interest in the conduct of research by the DHSS and MRC was Dr David Owen, as Minister of Health when Barbara Castle was at the helm. He was medically qualified, and had actually done some research before entering politics. His was the idea behind what I think is an interesting study which I did along with David Pole, later to become economic adviser to the DHSS. We were asked to quantitate what was loosely called "the burden of illness" of various types on the National Health Service. The International Classification of Disease (ICD) contained nearly 1000 categories of disease, which we boiled down to some 50 broad categories — such things as neoplasms (tumours), infections, heart attacks, and so on. We then set out the "burden" of each of these categories on the NHS, in terms of each of five indices: occupied beds; outpatient visits to hospital; general practitioner consultations; sickness benefit payments; and mortality, which we transmuted into loss of life expectancy.

As is not unknown in research, we rediscovered a number of obvious things — for example, that mental illness and handicap account for more than half the occupancy of hospital beds; and that more than half the loss of life expectancy can be accounted for by only three things out of 50 — heart attacks, neoplasms, and strokes. But these examples also show the weakness in this approach — if the main object were to empty beds, then one would give highest priority to mental illness; if to save life, to cardiovascular diseases and tumours. As mere civil servants, we could only average the burden derived from our five indices; it would take a politician, and a very brave one at that, to attach weightings to them. But if that were done it might be a better method of assessing service priorities than the random play of pressure groups. And of course as a determinant of priorities for research to be commissioned from the MRC (Dr Owen's original objective) it had the weakness that it took no account of "the state of the scientific art" — that is, the feasibility of a solution to the problem, and the availability of competent and interested scientists to tackle it.

When I entered the department my respect for politicians had ample room in which to grow; by the time I left it had done so, certainly at ministerial level. Ministers have to lead at least a triple life — dealing with their departmental responsibilities; political life in the House; and nursing their constituencies, including now for some the horrors of re-selection. They have my respect, and would indeed enjoy my sympathy if their wounds were not so obviously self inflicted.

Our national worship of the amateur reaches one of its most sacred peaks in the higher reaches of the administrative civil service. No matter how technical or scientific the concerns of a department may be, the recipe for choosing the captain of the ship is to take a first class Oxford (or, at a pinch, Cambridge) graduate, selected by competitive examination for entry to the administrative grade; cycle him through a minister's private office, then one of the central departments — Treasury, Cabinet Office, or Civil Service Department; then purge him of any particular expertise that he may have acquired by putting him at the head of a department in which he has never worked. Amazingly, the system succeeds — possibly because it achieves a fine balance of ignorance between senior politicians and civil servants, but more probably because of the intense selection, starting from excellent material, which ensures that only the most expert administrators reach the grade of deputy, let alone permanent, secretary. Another safeguard, possibly unintentional, is that by the time even a gifted civil servant has reached the top of the ladder, he is likely to be within five or six years of retirement.

The two permanent secretaries with whom I worked were Sir Philip Rogers and Sir Patrick Nairne. I was happy with both of them, and if either of them was unhappy with me he concealed it manfully. The external formality of civil servants is replaced within the circle by the general use of first names, used naturally and not forcedly as in a television interview. I still recall the exquisite tact with which this and similar matters were explained to me by Philip at our first or second meeting, even while my name was still going up for what must have been a rather formal sanction by Edward Heath. He also saw me through the kind of gaffe which someone who has spent years in one system, and acquired a measure of confidence, is liable to commit as a tiro in another system. When I entered the department I made the mistake of reading my job description (a mistake which I did not repeat on going to the Royal College of Physicians), and found that I was entitled to something termed "direct access to the Secretary of State." I had sense enough to divine that this was probably something to be used rather sparingly, but when some months later the first cut in research funding came along, I thought that the time had come. (After all, I had been appointed in the expectation of an expansion in research activity, and I felt like an Israelite in Egypt, required to make more bricks with less straw.) So I sent a solemn remonstrance, in the shape of a minute to Sir Keith Joseph. The roof remained on the building, so I imagine that my minute was intercepted in the private office; but I was made courteously aware that "direct" meant via the finance division and the permanent secretary. At the farewell dinner which his senior colleagues gave when Philip left the department, he feigned nostalgia for the old days in the civil service when a troublesome letter could be dismissed with the reply, "I am directed by the Secretary of State to inform you that your letter is not among those selected for a reply."

Philip had spent most of his civil service career in the Colonial Office, but had then served in Cabinet Office, Treasury, and Civil Service Department. Sir Patrick Nairne, coming from a military family, and with a first class degree in history, had spent almost his entire civil service career in the Admiralty and later the Ministry of Defence but had undergone the almost statutory spell in the Cabinet Office before coming to the DHSS. After leaving the service he returned to Oxford as master of St Catherine's College. In addition to being a fine painter, Pat is chairman of the Society of Italic Handwriting. Although this would lead me to suppose that in addition to his many other gifts he can write a fine Italian hand, the quality for which I most admire him is that of straightforwardness. It was this, I believe, that made him so open to accept Jim Gowans's plea for the independence of medical research from quasi-political direction. To these two men we owe it that the burdens on medical research in this country are simply those of straitened resources, no longer compounded by the Byzantine device of transferred funds.

In any large organisation the greatest personal problems are not with those who succeed, nor even with those who are content to fail, but rather with those who could well have succeeded had not some unfortunate turn of events deprived them of the opportunity. The difficulty in that generalisation arises from the unpredictable way in which people, apparently fit for a post, actually fill it — some rise to the opportunity, others have their incapacity belatedly revealed, like the emperor Galba, of whom Tacitus said he was "omnium consensu capax imperii, nisi imperasset" — judged by everyone fit to be emperor, if only he had not ruled. In the civil service hierarchy, there are deputy secretaries and under secretaries who appear well fitted to become permanent secretaries but who never get their chance. It is to the great credit of the service, and those who enter it, that whatever personal disappointments such men may feel it does not affect their devotion to duty — and make no mistake of it, the upper ranks of the civil service do work very hard and very responsibly.

The very excellence of these men (who of course include many women) creates a problem for departments such as the DHSS which depend heavily on in-house professional advice. This is a general problem for the civil service, and the Fulton committee some years ago tried to tackle it, by recommending the recruitment of more professionally trained people into the administrative civil service, and giving professionals comparable rank at all levels; for example, the chief medical officer has the grade of permanent secretary. My own observations suggest that the problem has not been completely solved — how many important problems are? Although similar problems arise in other professions — nursing, engineering, economics and social science — I am really only qualified to say something of the problems of the doctor working in a central civil service department. There are no great problems at the top — George Godber would have been outstanding in any company, and his deputies, of whom Henry Yellowlees succeeded him and John Reid became CMO in Scotland, were of comparable calibre. But lower down the problem has to be faced that the new medical graduate does not see himself carrying a CMO's baton. He is likely to seek professional advancement in other ways for a number of years, so when he does enter the civil service his administrative colleagues have had a long time already in which to learn the trade. When the medical officer of health had a clearly defined role, this was a good training ground for future medical civil servants; but community physicians have less clearly defined responsibilities, and the recent mystique of general managers will not help. Not I hope from any personal bias, I always had the view that there should be freer exchange of staff between the universities, the NHS, and the DHSS — so I was pleased when the present CMO, Sir Donald Acheson, was brought in from the university system; and doubly so when he undertook a review of the responsibilities of community physicians.

Coming to a more junior level in the medical staffing of the DHSS, I met another problem which stemmed from my dependence on the staff of the research division. To administer research with flair and efficiency calls for knowledge and experience, which can only be acquired after some years; but for their own career advancement doctors were advised to move through several divisions of the department. I sometimes felt that the DHSS doctors charged with managing research were at a disadvantage compared with those making their entire career with the MRC. Again, this did not apply at the top — Dick Cohen came from the MRC, and Max Wilson had spent many years in research management. Of course it is now almost 10 years since I left the DHSS, and things may have changed. I must also make it quite clear that I enjoyed, both personally and professionally, my contacts with the staff in research management.

Although I missed my clinical work, one of the fears with which I had entered the DHSS turned out to be exaggerated. I had dreaded loss of contact with my own profession and with the university system; but I was privileged in two ways: first, by my entry into the DHSS only after I was more or less established in my profession; and second, by discovering early on that a central part of my task was to maintain and even develop my previous contacts. Although external advisers can never replace in-house professional advice, they are very important in preventing professional isolation for the civil servant; and the CMO and his colleagues rightly have many channels for outside advice, with appointed advisers in all fields of medical activity. My own network had to be even more varied, if not wider; for it incorporated advisers from economics, social administration, and sociology, as well as from community medicine and workers in health service research. I enjoyed these wider contacts, and also learning, at the margin, some of the workings of a large department. In the university world I had not been entirely innocent of committees, but as chief scientist I had a triple ration of general DHSS committees, of internal research committees, and the council and boards of the MRC, since the CMO and the chief scientist became members of the MRC in 1973, the CMO having previously been an assessor. (I made it my business never to learn the difference between a member, an assessor, and an observer — since I firmly believe that any discussion which ends in a vote may be considered to have failed.) This brings me to some damaging admissions about committees.

First, and perhaps worst, I enjoy committees. Nearly 20 years ago, in the "Personal view" series of the *British Medical Journal*, I described the syndrome of committee insomnia — an inability to sleep soundly in committees. I confessed at the time that I was a victim of the syndrome, and I can now reveal that it has got worse, to the extent that I actually prefer chairing a committee to being a member — thereby virtually flinging away the opportunity of 40, or even 20 winks. My enjoyment does not always come from the business of the committee, which may even be quite dull, but from the interplay between members — perhaps I have found a substitute for that weighing up of the make up of patients which is so necessary a part of the practice of medicine.

Second, I do not pay too much attention, either in advance or at the meeting, to the minutes of the previous meeting. I scan them for obvious errors, of meaning rather than of grammar, but there is always someone who has honoured them with microscopic scrutiny, and for whom it will be a real pleasure to point out the misplaced comma or split infinitive. I have been at meetings (as a member) where discussion of the minutes of the previous meeting expanded to fill all the available time, and that cannot be good. The final report of a series of meetings is important — but a recipe for a bad report is to compile it as a compote of previous minutes, and not to write it ad hoc.

Third, and last of these confessions related to committees, when I am in the chair I don't worry too much about the agenda, though I do read it beforehand. Quite often, a vital member of the committee is constrained either to come late or to leave early — reprehensible, no doubt, but it is better to adjust the timing of the items to his availability than to have to deal with him by correspondence. And while it is certainly desirable to get to the end of an agenda, if some unforeseen matter should prolong (justifiably) an earlier discussion, it is surely better to postpone an item to a later meeting than to try to rush it through as people are getting their coats on.

I take the business of committees seriously, but not necessarily the conventions; and I always try to let cheerfulness break in, unless the solemnity of the occasion entirely precludes it. And I try to keep meetings short, since few people can concentrate for more than a couple of hours at a time.

By and large, the policy of a department is determined to some extent by the political considerations of ministers, or the activities of pressure groups — but mainly by the constraints, financial and other, of the real world. There was a management booklet in the DHSS in which someone had invented a tale of mystery and imagination in the form of a circle around which practical problems led to research initiatives, which in turn led to policy changes, which then had to be evaluated in the outside world by further research. This misleadingly clearcut scheme captured the imagination of some members of my chief scientists' committee, who then expressed a wish to influence the policy of the department. I reminded them of the definition of air travel as long periods of boredom punctuated by spasms of acute anxiety; and explained to them that departmental policy meant long periods of conventional wisdom, punctuated by spasms of political initiative. The conventional wisdom was largely a reflection of the real world. The basis of political initiatives is more interesting, and I struggled to discover it. The two things that I identified as stimulants to initiative, as opposed to reactive, DHSS activity were direct and repeated instructions by a minister, and the emergence of a parliamentary question which had not itself been stimulated on the initiative of the department.

Of course the devices by which policy was formed had to be complemented by measures designed to make policy acceptable first to parliament, and ultimately to the electorate. It was in this context that I learnt the three meanings of consultation. It is customary for any major government proposal to be put out initially in the form of a green paper, which is opened to public discussion before the final white paper is prepared to put before parliament, and ultimately to become first a bill, and then an act, if legislation is required. This opportunity for interested or affected parties to make representations corresponds to the dictionary meaning of consultation. But the meaning which may be attached to consultation is not limited to a genuine survey of opinion with a view of modifying a proposal.

The second meaning of consultation relates to a process by which the appearance of consultation is preserved, but there is no intention to modify the original proposal. When this type of pretend consultation has been carried through, it becomes possible to enrich a proposal with the phrase, "after wide consultation has been completed . . ." This type of pseudo-consultation does not rule out making minor changes in the proposal, so that its opponents cannot claim that nothing has been changed.

The third type of consultation is in some way analogous to the making of a self fulfilling prophecy. This consists in the appointment of a working group, or even a single adviser, to report on a proposition when it is already probable that the group or individual is likely to endorse it. I became aware of this ploy when ministers were for some reason anxious to delegate certain responsibilities from the DHSS itself to the regional health authorities; they sought the advice of selected chairmen of these authorities, and should not have been too surprised when the right answer came back. A more recent, and still more serious, example came when the government, no doubt spellbound by the triumphs of British industrial management, came to the conclusion that this was the way to run a health service. Whom should they ask to advise them in this matter, but a top manager in a large grocery business; and he too came up with the expected answer. Fortunately perhaps, the method does not always work, and that splendid national institution the BBC had an unexpected reprieve from a forced introduction of commercialism.

Since this is not a chronology, I would like to digress to describe my only meeting with the author of the Griffiths report on management in the health service. The Association for the Study of Medical Education held a meeting on management, and I was asked to take the chair for the morning session. The first speaker was Mr Griffiths himself, scheduled to speak for 20 minutes. He did in fact speak for 30 minutes, including a statement that at 8 am that morning he knew where every one of his lorries was placed. At the end of this, and perhaps feeling embarrassed by my failure to stop him on time, I said that although the 10 minutes allotted for discussion had already passed, through my fault, Mr Griffiths was nevertheless the principal speaker, and we should therefore still have 10 minutes of discussion. This produced a complete silence, and I had to rush in once again, which I did by asking about one of the main points in his proposals, that senior people should be recruited from industrial management to take up managerial positions in the NHS. I suggested that it was possible that such recruits might not be the people whom the industries would most want to keep, but rather those whom, possibly after 20 years of business lunches, they were anxious to lose. By the time he had dismissed this hypothesis the silence had been broken. But I still feel I missed a trick —I should have asked him what use he made of the information about the lorries.

The concluding section of this chapter is also anachronistic, as it relates to an activity which indeed began while I was still in the DHSS, but which continued for three years after I left, and indeed still concerns me; but my comments on inequalities in health more properly form a part of this chapter, than of the next. This is not the place to summarise the report of our working group, which has been made widely available in the Pelican edition, with a foreword by Peter Townsend and Nick Davidson. What I want to do here is to describe our working method, and say something of the subsequent story of the report.

If a working group or party is actually going to do any work, it should be small; and if it is to come to reasonable conclusions, it must be balanced in its membership. We were indeed fortunate that we were able to achieve a reasonable balance, in a membership of only four; but of course we also had the backing of two research assistants and the secretariat of the DHSS. To support my contention that we were balanced (which might conceivably be challenged from right of centre), I would say that we had two doctors (Jerry Morris and myself) and two sociologists (Cyril Smith and Peter Townsend). Going further, there was balance within each of these broad disciplines — Professor J N Morris being in social medicine and epidemiology, while I am at heart a clinician; Peter Townsend, a national expert on poverty and deprivation, can I think be described as fairly radical, while Cyril Smith, then secretary of the Social Science Research Council would I think join me as a conservative with a rather small "c"; we were also rather more taciturn than the two enthusiasts. Although we all worked well together, our task was complicated, and there was also a bit of a tussle between those (like myself) who wanted to get something out, and others (particularly Jerry Morris) who wanted rewrites to incorporate the latest figures. We had many meetings, spread over three years; and by the time we finished, in 1980, the government had changed the year before and Patrick Jenkin had succeeded David Ennals at the DHSS.

The report provided further detailed evidence of the health disadvantage suffered by manual workers, particularly the unskilled, and we put the main blame for this on their relative lack of resources. We also contended that it was general social deprivation rather than anything specifically related to the NHS, or access to it, which was mainly responsible. A radical cure for the problem would clearly be expensive. For all of these reasons our report must have been unpalatable to a government that was not in any case keen on public expenditure, or on specific measures to alleviate poverty and its effects. It was, of course, fair comment that the world contains other examples of inequality in health of roughly the same magnitude, between men and women; or of distinctly greater magnitude, between the developed and developing nations. My colleagues and I were not, however, reconciled to the idea that the existence of other types of health inequality removed the need for doing something about the one which lay to hand, and was at least partially remediable.

Although the DHSS brought out the report in an unwieldy form and a limited edition towards the end of August 1980, I do not myself share the view that this was a conscious effort at suppression. It may I suppose have been subconscious, a thing which is difficult either to prove or disprove. But if — against my own belief — there was any such intention, it certainly failed. Even before the Pelican edition gave the report wide currency, there were countless seminars and discussions on it with, as one would expect, a particular welcome from politicians in opposition, from health service workers, and from paediatricians, since we had advocated special measures to improve the health of the children of manual workers. And of course the problems themselves have not gone away, as the most recent figures show, and as awareness has increased of the health risks associated with unemployment.

I believe that we were right in our main (and also most controversial) contention, that the relatively high morbidity and mortality experienced by manual workers was the consequence of social deprivation, and not the other way round. It has been argued against this that a rather ill defined condition, designated as failure to cope, leads both to ill health and to low social status. If someone some day should discover a cure for failure to cope, I would of course welcome it; but for the present I will not give up hope that alleviating poverty and its effects might more directly benefit health.

Probably my colleagues would not agree, but I think we got one aspect rather out of perspective. I believe we may have accepted rather too uncritically the current belief, supported particularly by my friend Tom McKeown and others, that the improvement in health which has taken place over the past 150 years has been overwhelmingly due to social factors — sanitation, housing, and better nutrition and only marginally to curative medicine. As a clinician living through the "therapeutic revolution," I never found this easy to accept, but there was little evidence available to confute it. Some evidence is now being reported, on the lines that mortality from diseases for which treatment is effective is declining more rapidly than mortality from diseases which are still without effective treatment. This certainly does not conflict with common sense; but it is not easy to reconcile with the idea that social factors are infinitely more important than therapeutic intervention.

6 11 St Andrews Place (1977-83)

The drive towards healthy living and the drive towards convenience and pleasure do not always push in the same direction. It is obviously convenient to have the workplace and the home in the same building, and pleasant to "dine out" once or twice a week without having to cross the threshold; but these are not prescriptions for the weight watcher. I still think I was very fortunate to enjoy them — even if only for one period of six years — in a life which more generally afforded me the doubtful pleasures of commuting from a suburban home to work in the centre of cities. How did my holiday from daily travel come about? Like so many things, indirectly.

At the instance of Thomas Linacre, physician and classical scholar, Henry VIII founded the Royal College of Physicians in 1518, when he was still only 27, capable of good works and open to reason. In those days physicians were an élite within the profession, graduates of Oxford or Cambridge, and commonly also of Padua, like Linacre himself and in a later generation William Harvey. The three volumes of college history, by Sir George Clark and Dr A M Cooke, describe the rivalries between the physicians and the apothecaries, and within the college itself between the fellows, who monopolised the governance of the college, and the licentiates. It cannot have been easy to define a physician when it was a matter of status rather than of function, and it remains difficult for a lay person to understand the distinction between a physician and a general practitioner. The role of the surgeon is well understood, at least in general terms; but the idea of a specialist who does not operate is less easy to explain. It may be easier in America, where they use the terms internal medicine and internist; but I suspect that even there physicians are confused with interns. Even 50 years ago membership of the Royal College of Physicians was a natural higher qualification for pathologists, psychiatrists, and family doctors as well as for physicians in the strict sense. As colleges have been established in these disciplines, and also in radiology, the diploma of MRCP is perhaps less sought after as a general qualification now that alternatives are more freely available

The great benefits that have come from increased specialisation, and in particular from incorporation of the developing specialties in new colleges and faculties, have carried a certain cost in the fragmentation of medicine, but only an overindulgent nostalgia would claim that the loss has exceeded the gains. And of course the college still welcomes into its membership, or indeed its fellowship, people who have distinguished themselves in other branches of medicine or surgery. Three times a year, new members are formally admitted to the college, both those specially elected, and also the much more numerous band of those who have obtained this diploma by a rather stiff examination, taken a few years after qualification in medicine. When I had the privilege of admitting new members I was able to tell them that all the college officers had obtained their membership in the hard way, by examination; and at the dinner in the evening I would encourage them by saying that they had probably just surmounted the most difficult hurdle on the way to becoming president. I am not sure that they believed me, any more than I would have done had Robert Hutchison said the same thing to me in 1939 when I got my MRCP.

The college was then in its fourth home, in a porticoed building in Pall Mall overlooking Trafalgar Square, and known to taxi drivers as "the dirty end of Canada House." It was not a place of common and friendly resort, and members then played no part in the affairs of the college. I did not pass the porter in his chair in the hallway between being admitted a member (no dinner in those days), and being admitted a fellow in 1952. Things speeded up a little after that, and in the following year I gave the Goulstonian lectures (some years earlier, my Cambridge chief R A McCance had given three lectures, by my time it was down to two, and now it is a single lecture, but still given by one of the four youngest new fellows). The facilities are better now, in the new college — in my day the lectures were given accompanied by the hissing of a carbon arc, which may have been fair comment. Attendances are better now also — when I gave them, the bulk of the audience were the dozen or so college officers, together with a beadle who had the useful gift of apparent slumber during the lecture, but instant wakefulness when the time came for him to shoulder the mace. There was also a younger fellows' club with access to the president, Russell Brain; and the privilege of attending the quarterly meetings of the college, known as comitia. I gave further college lectures on kidney problems, the Bradshaw in 1965 and the Lumleian in 1970, but during my time in Manchester I really played very little part in college affairs, even though in one particular way I was kept well in touch with them.

Russell Brain demitted the presidency in 1957, and Robert Platt was elected to succeed him and held office for a period of five years, during which it is not too much to say that the college changed course in such a way as to make it a truly national body, with two main foci of interest: the training and certification of physicians and their appointment to posts in the NHS; and the maintenance of standards of practice in the interests of patients. These were not of course entirely new objectives, but the limited accommodation in Pall Mall East effectively prevented their adequate development—no proper lecture rooms or committee rooms, and nowhere to house supporting secretarial staff in sufficient numbers. Steps were taken to secure accommodation appropriate to a modern college, and to develop a programme of postgraduate teaching going far beyond the occasional named lecture. For the first of these, negotiation with the Canadian government secured a substantial sum of money for the existing building, Sir Isaac Wolfson provided

88

further large sums, and Denys Lasdun was commissioned to design a worthy modern building in Regent's Park. For the second, the post of assistant registrar was created, with the specific responsibility of developing postgraduate training, and in particular a regular advanced course in medicine; the first holder of this post was a keen young physician, Nigel Compston, who was later, as a keen older physician, to play a cardinal role as treasurer in a further phase of college expansion. These things took time, and the new building was not opened until after Robert Platt had in turn demitted office, but it was during his time that these vital decisions were taken, in which the registrar, Sir Kenneth Robson, and the treasurer, Dr Dick Bomford, also played an essential part.

I was not directly concerned, except as an ordinary fellow, with any of this; but as Robert Platt still worked in the same hospital, we did have a lot of informal discussion about the future activities of the college. Relevant also to my own future, little though I would have suspected it at the time, was the fact that Robert was the first full time academic physician to be elected president, and also the first from the provinces—a splendid imperial proconsular phrase. When Max Rosenheim, another nephrologist and general physician, became president a few years later, I was again well informed on college affairs; and when I moved down to the DHSS in 1973 I was able to attend college meetings more regularly. In 1976 I held college office for the first time in the post of second vice president, which carried a seat in the college council, and occasional deputising for the president, Sir Cyril Clarke (when Harry Himsworth was second vice president a few years earlier, and someone inconsiderately asked him what the duties were, he said "to be a second stomach for Max"). The first or senior vice president, also called the senior censor, holds a much more onerous responsibility, being in charge of the examination, held three times a year, in which several hundred candidates are in search of membership of the college — also, as the registrar would later remind me, if a president should die in office, the senior vice president succeeds him until an election is held at the normal time. For the examination, he is of course assisted by three other censors, and three pro-censors, as well as a number of additional examiners.

During my period as vice president, Cyril Clarke made it known that he would not be seeking re-election as president in the spring of 1977; and I also became aware that I was among those who were being considered by fellows as a possible president. I had of course attended previous elections, which are generally rather formal when it is known that the president wishes to continue, but are more interesting when a new president is to be elected. In college terms, a procedure which only dates back to the last century has to be considered innovative, but as innovations go it has lasted a long time. The election is held on the Monday after Palm Sunday each year, at 4 30 pm. Each fellow present is given a piece of paper, on which he writes a single name, that of a fellow of 10 years' standing whom he considers appropriate to be president. The papers are collected, and the senior censor, becoming increasingly hoarse, reads out the names, while a tally is kept. If a fellow gets two thirds of the votes he is elected; and this is what generally happens in the year of a formal election, when the president wishes to continue. However, when there is a real decision to be made, and when of course many different names are likely to be put forward, a two thirds majority is rarely obtained. Blank papers are again distributed, and the fellows are asked to enter the name of one of only two candidates, those who came first and second in the previous ballot. The papers are collected and given to the senior censor who reads out the names once again; this time election is by a simple majority, even by a single vote. (On one occasion the senior censor was one of the remaining two candidates, and fortunately the successful one — it would have been heart breaking to read all these names, including one's own, and still lose.)

In 1977 the election fell on 4 April, and as one of the college officers I was seated facing the mass of fellows, of whom several hundred had turned up. Frankly, I wanted to be elected, but was not hopeful of being so; and I kept an unofficial tally of the votes, not through coolness, but to have something to do. When I was still in after the first ballot, I realised things were serious. The various college officers had been given cards saying what their duties were — "Collect papers"; "Pass urns to the senior censor"; "Maintain a tally" and so on. As I was known to be a candidate, my directions were simple: "Remain seated." This was not, however, adequate preparation for what turned out to be my election as president, and I was sufficiently confused to dissolve the meeting before taking the oath which qualified me to do so.

I am naturally biased in favour of a procedure which gave me six very happy and responsible years, but the system has its critics. The main objections are that fellows in London have an advantage of convenience over those in the rest of the country, and also overseas; and that fellows have no means of knowing which fellows are in the running. The first objection led to the proposal that election should be by postal vote and not limited to those actually attending; this was countered by the claim that those sufficiently concerned to attend would constitute a better electoral college than the mass of fellows, many of whom were overseas. The second objection can be met by a less radical proposal, that of requiring formal nomination of candidates. It seems likely that the idea of a postal vote will be rejected, for the period at least; but the nomination procedure is likely to be introduced.

The DHSS is not the first love of every physician in the land; and my being a hireling of that institution contributed to my surprise at being elected. I was not the only person to be surprised, for an editorial in the journal *World Medicine* criticised the college for enjoying "too cosy a relationship with the mandarins at the Department of Health"; and suggested that I had "stepped off with the wrong foot" by not giving up my DHSS post immediately. I was, however, consoled by the thought that the best time to make mistakes is at the beginning of a new venture. In clinical medicine one lives perforce with a good deal of uncertainty, and this may be quite a good preparation for living with a certain amount of ambiguity. And that there might be ambiguity I discovered fairly rapidly.

The new president takes up office immediately on election; and as it happened the very next day was set for the meeting of a body known as the joint consultants committee (JCC for short). This is a group of consultants drawn in equal numbers from the British Medical Association, through the central committee for hospital medical services (CCHMS); and from the conference of royal colleges and faculties. The JCC represents in a general way the views of consultants, but it is not a negotiating body with the DHSS, that role being reserved for the BMA through its negotiating committee. Again in very general terms, the CCHMS members were legitimately concerned with terms and conditions of service and the college members with stand-ards of training and practice. These different aspects of the work of consultants are not rigidly separate, and the JCC was at its most effective when its two wings were making common cause. At the first meeting which I attended it seemed to me that the most potent unifying agent was common dislike of proposals from the DHSS. I further noticed that in the morning session (attended only by the JCC and the secretariat) their dislike was expressed freely, even flamboyantly; but in the afternoon session when the JCC were joined by the chief medical officer and a number of his henchmen, the proceedings were toned down to some extent. My own position was somewhat piquant. My re-search responsibilities in the DHSS never impinged on the areas covered by the JCC, so I was seeing them in action for the first time; also, I was still formally on secondment to the DHSS, which gave me a reason for staying rather quiet — and also a rationalisation, for I am not a natural medical politician. I did not find my first meeting of the JCC particularly enjoyable, but as time passed I was quite glad to have been thrown in at the deep end.

The conference of royal colleges and faculties was a different matter. It is made up of the presidents or deans of the various colleges and faculties, in Scotland and Ireland as well as in England. The conference met four times a year, and rotated round the different colleges, mostly in London. I already knew a good many of the members of the group, and welcomed the opportunity to know more of them. I have a fondness for bodies which have influence rather than commanding authority; and I think this was the case with the conference, which had a chairman and secretary on an honorary basis but no administrative secretariat of its own. When there was a strong chairman, as Rodney Smith was, pronouncements could be conjured out of the conference on matters of general interest, such as brain death. But the main function of the group was to provide an opportunity for the representatives of the various colleges to bring forward their particular problems, on which a general college view could quite often be expressed. Obviously, at times the different colleges had different interests, and it was both a weakness and a strength of the conference that its views were informal, and not mandatory on its individual constituents.

But my main responsibility was to my own college, and only secondarily to the corporate bodies on which it was represented. The ultimate governing body of the college is the quarterly meeting or comitia; and any major decisions have to be ratified (or overturned) by that body. It is also possible for the college officers, or a sufficient number of fellows, to call for a special meeting of the college at times other than those set for the regular comitia. Any fellow of the college can attend comitia, join in the discussion, and vote on any matter. This prescription for democracy is of course limited by practicality; issues have to be formulated in such a way that decisions on them are actually possible within a finite framework of discussion. This important task of preliminary definition of a problem can be done in various ways. The college has an elected council, which can make recommendations to comitia. There is also a smaller body, the censor's board, made up of the censors and pro-censors, together with the president, registrar and assistant registrar; its main function is to conduct the MRCP examination, but it also meets on the morning of comitia, and can express a view in its report to comitia. None of these bodies is in continuous session, and interim decisions have to be taken by the president, with the advice of the college officers. These are the registrar, the treasurer, the senior censor, and the assistant registrar — there are other college officers, but they do not regularly attend the informal meetings at which the president ventilates college affairs and seeks advice.

As the college is concerned with the problems of physicians throughout England, Wales, and Northern Ireland, it is important that its decisions should not reflect only the views of physicians who practise in London and are therefore more likely to attend meetings regularly. During his tenure of the presidency Max Rosenheim saw this need, and in order to meet it he instituted the system of regional advisers — two from each of the NHS regions of the country. They meet on the morning of comitia, after the meeting of the censor's board, and in presenting issues to comitia the president takes account of the views which they express — and if he misinterprets them they can point this out at comitia. There is one further important source of advice for the college and its officers which should be mentioned — the specialist committees. There are over 20 different specialities within internal medicine, with different needs and perspectives that should be taken into account; in the college there are separate committees of cardiologists, gastroenterologists, and so on who can not only make recommendations on matters concerning their particular specialty but can also make representations on more general issues. (To give a specific example, the prevention of coronary heart disease is something which concerns all practising physicians, but it is a special preoccupation of cardiologists. When this was debated in comitia, it was important to have available, as part of the evidence, the considered view of the committee on cardiology.)

My justification for giving what may have been a tedious account of the mechanisms available to the college for making decisions is this: some understanding of them is necessary before I go on to try to answer two important questions — What are they for? and How do they work?

Imitation is said to be the sincerest form of flattery. But when imitation entails a considerable expenditure of effort, time, and money by numbers of individuals, it is safe to conclude that the imitation goes far beyond flattery, and betokens the recognition of a real need and function. The college system has spread from its sixteenth century beginnings in this country to Australia and Canada, Singapore and Malaysia, as well as to the Union of South Africa and the United States of America; moreover, as the different branches of medicine have developed, colleges have been established in several disciplines other than that of a physician. My own views of the functions of a college have naturally been influenced by experience of the college which I know best; but I think they do apply in some measure to similar bodies in this country and abroad. There are several important negative characteristics or marks of a medical college — it is independent of government and not a creature of the state; it is not a negotiating body for its members on terms and conditions of service; it is not, at least primarily, a disciplinary body whose disapproval can be signalled by the imposition of penalties. (Although at one time the president of the Royal College of Physicians had the power to imprison a member for contumacious conduct, this does not appear to have been exercised, and may be said to have lapsed.) There remain on the statute book fines for members of certain bodies who fail to attend, without having obtained permission to be absent, but these again were seldom if ever exacted. The only sanction that is occasionally employed is to remove the college diploma from a member or fellow whose name has been removed from the Medical Register.

These limitations of function, which may appear as weaknesses, are in my view actually sources of strength. Independence from government in no way precludes the giving of advice to government, either when asked to do so or spontaneously, and the independence of the advice so given enhances its quality. Detachment from negotiations on the payment of physicians is a further and different source of independence in the expressed views of a college. And the lack of dependence on formal sanctions, such as might be necessary in the governance of children or potential criminals, should actually strengthen the authority of a corporation dealing with established professionally qualified adults.

Turning to the positive aims of a college, the over-riding one must be to maintain and improve the quality and standards of practice in the relevant branch of medicine; and to do this not as an exercise in professional aggrandisement or material advantage, but in the interests of patients. This aim can be achieved in part, and it is an important part, by fostering the individual professional training and skills of the members of the college, but any branch of a profession has to be practised within the framework of the profession as a whole, and beyond that within society. The particular responsibilities of a college of physicians must thus include the training, appointment, and continuing education of physicians, but must also go beyond that to a concern with the status of medicine as a whole, and with matters which influence the health of the public.

The General Medical Council claims responsibility for validating the entire education of a doctor from the time when he enters medical school to the time when he gives up practice. The implementation of this responsibility is, however, divided between two systems — the university system for the undergraduate training and to some extent the first year after qualification; and thereafter the college system for postgraduate training and continuing education. This division of responsibility between the university system and the colleges may look untidy, but I believe it is well justified, when one looks at the variety of careers open to a medical man. Five or six years in a university provide the opportunity to experience a wide variety of cultures, and to associate with people pursuing completely different courses of study; the student who grasps these opportunities should emerge with a degree of intellectual flexibility that should prepare him to cope with the considerable changes in medical knowledge and practice which are certain to occur in his lifetime of practice. (It may be an exaggeration to say that half of what we learn in medical school will be proved wrong in 50 years, and we don't know which half — but it is not a total travesty.) And even within medicine it is surely a good thing for the future physician to rub shoulders with those who will become surgeons, or pathologists, or public health doctors, and perhaps particularly with those who will enter general practice.

Nevertheless, when the young doctor has settled on his own choice of career — preferably after looking at several options, and in the light of advice — there is a degree of change in his educational requirements. While he must still conserve the breadth of mind which he should have acquired in his earlier training, it is now also incumbent on him to acquire in depth a particular framework of knowledge, aptitudes, and skills which is appropriate to his chosen specialty. The educational agency appropriate to such an enterprise is in my view not the *studium generale* of a university but a professional association dedicated to the particular discipline of the young doctor's choice. A training focused on the particular skills of a physician is best supervised by those who have themselves experienced such a training, and who continue to practise the corresponding branch — and this applies also to general practice and the other specialties.

I said at the beginning of this section that there were two questions relating to the functions of a college — What are they? and How does it perform them? Perhaps before I proceed to the more general functions of my own college, I should say a little of the mechanisms by which it carries out the educational function that I have just outlined.

The training of the future physician is naturally carried out in junior posts attached to medical units, and it is important in the public interest, as well as in the trainee's, to make sure that the post offers a suitable range of actual experience, as well as general facilities for theoretical study. This can only be ascertained by competent observers visiting the hospital, and making the appropriate inquiries relating to the individual post. The colleges have the responsibility of nominating the members of these visiting groups, and all posts of senior house officer, registrar, and senior registrar which are recognised for training purposes have been so inspected. The visiting group has simply to decide whether the post satisfies the requirements for providing adequate training; above that level, we have uniformly resisted proposals that posts should be graded — to do so would greatly prejudice the local cooperation that we have generally enjoyed, and it would be all too easy for politicians or administrators to shift the odium for closing down a post on other grounds to a specious educational reason. A health authority is naturally anxious to obtain the best people to fill its junior posts, and recognition for training purposes is very influential in this context; when a visiting party offers recognition for training subject to certain conditions, such as improved library facilities or an alteration in duties, this can be quite a powerful lever in persuading authorities towards improvements. The recognition, and where necessary the upgrading of posts, has to be supplemented by assessment of the overall experience of the individual trainees; when this is satisfactory it leads to accreditation as a physician, which is usually only obtained some 8 to 10 years after qualifying; some of the terminology which has become current is rather misleading — junior is scarcely apposite to a man in his mid-thirties, and registrar may suggest someone whose skills are limited to the use of a notebook and pencil.

The college has put a great deal of effort into the supervision of training posts and individual programmes leading towards accreditation. These efforts have not, however, earned universal approbation — which may be an indication that the colleges have actually done something. There is an underlying tension between securing a minimum standard of practice, which the public rightly demands, and conserving the variety and flexibility of training which will combine proper practical experience with opportunities for research, for experience overseas, or a period in general practice. The view from the centre, held as it often is by those who have made their way through a varied rather than a stereotyped career, tends to emphasise flexibility; but the bodies which adjudicate on accreditation in particular specialties within medicine sometimes contain people who lean towards a concentration on what they see as relevant experience rather than on greater diversity of experience.

As the future consultant physician approaches the end of his training, he begins to apply for appropriate tenured posts. The college is represented on all the committees for the appointment of consultants in medicine or a medical specialty. Although the representative of the college does not have a veto, he has an important voice both in advising on whether the training of the candidate has been adequate, and also in ensuring that candidates are considered on their merits and not on whether they have conformed to a rigid pattern of experience obtained over a stereotyped period of time. Recommendations for both the length and the content of training are guidelines and not regulations; if a candidate is otherwise well fitted for a post, the fact that he has not yet fulfilled all the requirements set out for accreditation is not an absolute bar. Some people learn much more quickly than others, so the notional four years of higher medical training should not be regarded as a *sine qua non*; and if the candidate seems ideal in all other respects, but lacks some particular type of expertise, the correct course is surely to make a delayed appointment, while he gains that particular skill, rather than to pass him over for someone less generally suitable. The college representative has another function which is important, even if he rarely has to exercise it fully: some members of some committees tend to give undue weight to local factors, or even local prejudices; the college representative, who always comes from another region, can counterbalance this, and what he says should carry weight; but if he suspects that serious favouritism or nepotism has entered into the selection, he can complain to the registrar of the college, who can then take up a sufficiently serious matter with the regional health authority or with the DHSS.

The college holds very strongly the view that a consultant appointment does not mean the end of medical education, but rather a new beginning, spurred on by increased opportunity and responsiblity. It is generally recognised that coming together for conferences is an important part of continuing education, and the college, as well as many other bodies, organises these both regionally and nationally. The specialist committees of the college also try to ensure that local conditions of staffing, accommodation, and equipment are such as to permit good medical practice.

Throughout its history the college has from time to time looked beyond the sectional interests of physicians to a concern with the public health. True, it was not with the complete approval of the college that Culpeper in 1649 published an English translation of the college's Latin pharmacopoeia. Early in the eighteenth century, however, the college spoke out against the widespread drunkenness in society, and recommended an increase in the duty on spirits; the extent to which subsequent governments have followed this recommendation stands in some contrast to their response to comparable recommendations on the smoking of cigarettes.

These general concerns of the college have certainly not been neglected in recent years. The most notable series of recent reports is surely that on the risks taken by smokers. The first of these, *Smoking and Health*, was published in 1962; the second and third in 1971 and 1977; and the most recent, *Health or Smoking?* in 1983. Not long before I succeeded Cyril Clarke as president, a report was issued recommending the addition of small amounts of fluoride to the water supply to lessen the risk of dental caries; although I was not concerned in the preparation of the report, I had to deal with the considerable correspondence which followed it. During my own time at the college we had three working parties on nutritional topics: dietary fibre, obesity, and food intolerance. Also, two on the problems of the elderly: mental impairment, and the particular problems of medication for older people. We also had reports on health services for those undergoing higher education, and on death certification — superficially perhaps a gloomy topic, but of great importance in maintaining the salutary scrutiny of medical practice, and as a basis for many important studies in epidemiology, such as the association between smoking and lung cancer.

Anyone who raises his head, or has it raised, above the parapet which in general protects us from publicity must expect the occasional rough ride from the media, and also from individual correspondents. My own experience in this kind has been varied, and perhaps not devoid of interest. I am not referring to the many supportive letters and comments which I have received from time to time — grateful though I am for them, good news scarcely seems to count as interesting news.

I think the topic on which I have received the greatest number of hostile letters from the general public is fluoridation. This may be partly artificial, as much of the correspondence was clearly orchestrated by organised pressure groups. My most memorable individual experience came when I was unwise enough to take part in a phone-in radio programme; someone rang in with statements on fluoride, couched in the form of questions. The compère had obviously had previous experience of this, for he passed over to me a slip of paper on which he had written, "Another fluoride nut."

A few MPs seem to be particularly sensitive to attempts to influence their views on smoking. I have actually been threatened with being reported to the Speaker for breach of parliamentary privilege. I have also been stigmatised as a "do-gooder." Since the alternatives to being a do-gooder are presumably to be a "do-nothinger" or a "do-badder," I treat such responses with equanimity.

I have once had the interesting experience of being publicly hissed. I was speaking at a meeting of the London forum on inequalities in health; when it came to the discussion period a lady in the audience made a general appeal, not arising from anything I had said, to "march to Trafalgar Square, and demand the immediate removal of lead from petrol." I should have held my peace — there was no need to reply. But instead when I hinted that the evidence incriminating lead in petrol as the root of all evil was not entirely conclusive, a considerable section of the audience, sitting together as a group, expressed their disapproval.

I happened to be chairman of the conference of royal

colleges and faculties at the time of the *Panorama* programme on brain death in the winter of 1980-1. On evidence largely derived from experience in America, this programme caused considerable public anxiety about the criteria in use in this country for establishing brain death as a prerequisite for discontinuing life support systems. They also set this in the context of obtaining organs for transplantation, whereas the main reason for employing valid criteria of brain death is to spare relatives the futile agony of watching someone dear to them die a slow inevitable death over a period of days or even weeks. Isolated tests carried out on a single occasion by an isolated individual are of course fallible, but any decision to invoke brain death, and to take action thereon, is taken in the light of the whole clinical picture, by teams of experienced people, none of whom is connected with the possible use of organs for transplantation. The programme and the reaction to it alerted me to the distinction between those sections of the media concerned with topicality and those with an informed interest in scientific matters.

My most recent dealings with the media have been in the context of the possible association of nuclear emissions at Sellafield with childhood leukaemia in Seascale. My reluctance to equate association with causality seems to me to be proper scientific scepticism, but to some sections of the media failure to progress from possibility through probability to certainty appears as sheer pig headedness. Any sensible citizen must have some concern about the way in which unacknowledged leaks of radioactivity became known after many years, but that is not a problem to which I have any expert contribution to make. When asked about one such incident, with a view to my appearing on a programme, I elicited that the leak was almost certainly a small one, and that it involved an isotope which was known to cause thyroid cancer rather than leukaemia. At the end of our telephone conversation my interrogator said, with sadness in his voice, "You've killed my interest in the story."

After that digression on assorted encounters with the media, I would make the claim that the system whereby the college acts through working parties to produce reports is a valuable one, and it continues to be active. Some account of how the process works may thus be worth while, although the details differ from one working party to the next. Suggestions for appropriate topics for future reports are made by individuals within the college, by the committees of the college, and also in response to representations from the DHSS or from other outside bodies. These suggestions are considered by the governing bodies in the college, the main constraint being the number of groups that can sensibly be active at any one time. After all, the membership of the working groups is going to be drawn from people who are likely to be occupied in many other ways, because of the very expertise which qualifies them to be members of the college group.

There is no problem about selecting the chairman of a working group — the president chairs them all, and I suppose that may count as another proper limit on their numbers. The lay secretariat is provided from within the college, and it is usual to find a scientific secretary from among the group. Some 15 to 20 members, drawn from different disciplines but always including a high proportion of fellows and members of the college, are asked to serve, and are almost always willing to do so. Since topics appropriate for a working group are almost all many sided, there is a choice between trying to get the various relevant disciplines represented on the working party or leaving some areas of discourse to be covered by interviewing experts in particular topics. In the college arrangement the general aim is the first of these, to cover the subject as much as possible from inside the group, though it is also possible for the group to meet non-members of the group with particular interests. This method, in which a scientific secretary collates contributions from within the group, contrasts with another feasible method in which experts outside the group are commissioned to write sections of a report, which is then simply discussed by a predominantly generalist working party. Both systems have advantages and disadvantages; I have some preference, probably bias, for the college method, even though it means more work for the members of the group.

When the report has been prepared, which usually takes some 12 to 18 months of intermittent activity, it has to be approved by council and comitia before being published as a college report. Publication is either in the college journal, or as a separate document; and the issue of the report is generally the subject of a press conference, chaired by the president and attended by available members of the working group.

I have gone into some detail in describing the educational and the general activities of the college because they are not so generally known as I believe they deserve to be. What I have not indicated, except perhaps by implication, is the quite remarkable willingness of very busy people to assist the college in these various ways; and also how enjoyable the various college activities are. I think I can say with some authority that the college is what is called a happy ship — it was so before I came to it, and continues to be so now that I have left it, but I look back on my period there as one of the happiest in my life. The naval metaphor is not inappropriate, for the secretary of the college for the past two decades was in submarines during the war. Michael Tibbs has contributed greatly to both the humanity and the efficiency of the administration of the college, and all done with grace and lightness of touch.

Although the day to day running of the college is done by the secretary and his staff on a full time basis, many of the activities of the college require medical professional expertise, and this is provided by some hundreds of doctors who act as examiners, take part in visits, serve on committees, and lecture in conferences. The central coordination of these activities also requires a medical input, and for this the president, on whose frail shoulders ultimate responsibility rests between quarterly meetings, relies mainly on the treasurer and registrar, who hold office for a number of years, but also on the senior censor for that year. The assistant registrar, whose primary responsibility is for organising the educational programme, is also an important and regular source of advice. Since corporations such as the college in the end depend on the people who run them, and since my senior colleagues made my tenure of the office of president so happy for me, I will close my account of the college years by saying something of their contribution.

Throughout my period of office, and for some years before, the treasurer was Dr Nigel Compston, physician to the Royal Free Hospital, editor of successive editions of *Recent Advances in Medicine*, and former assistant registrar of the college. The treasurer is responsible for the buildings of the college, and its properties and finance, and is also one of the president's two most regular and senior advisers. But the most notable and permanent of Nigel's achievements must surely be the acquisition by the college of the Nash buildings surrounding St Andrews Place. I headed this chapter "11 St Andrews Place," for that was the address of the college when I entered and left it. But it could more properly now be 1-11 St Andrews Place, for a single building, admittedly an important one designed by Sir Denys Lasdun, has now become a medical precinct. (I happened to be standing next to Sir Denys when the precinct was opened by the Queen in the summer of 1986, and remarked to him that in view of our respective professions we might be escaping lightly in being presented to the Queen rather than to her eldest son, whom, however, I had the great honour of admitting to the fellowship of our college.) The acquisition of the precinct, however happy, can scarcely be described as a happy stroke; for it took all of a dozen years of patient negotiation by Nigel Compston and Michael Tibbs. During those years hopes rose and fell as possible developers of the south east corner of Regent's Park in turn appeared and in turn faded away. But in the end a fine urban enclave allows Nigel and Michael to say, if they would, not only *Finis coronat opus*, but also *Si monumentum requiris, circumspice*.

My other senior colleague, the registrar, was David Pyke, known to and loved by hundreds of fellows and members of the college, and many others besides. Third in a notable sequence of physicians looking after diabetic patients in King's College Hospital, he was for a time secretary of the Association of Physicians, an office which entails writing up on the board the names of those physicians who rise to take part in discussion. There can be no better training for carrying out the assortative mating of names and faces which I personally find so elusive, and David has continued to build on this sound foundation. He contributes each quarter "Notes from the registar" to the college commentary; if there is a more penetrating and amusing commentator on the passing medical scene I would like to read him, but have not yet done so. I have confessed earlier that I am not a stickler for administration, and I have also recounted David's contribution to curing me from my addiction to the tobacco pipe. As others have done, he kept me just within the bounds of administrative propriety; and I have never been guided with a gentler rein.

I was marvellously fortunate in having throughout my period both Nigel and David — who were in some ways complementary to each other in qualities — but my good fortune did not end there. As it happened, there were three assistant registrars during my six years of office, all of them excellent. Jim Malpas was just reaching the end of his stint, and Robert Boyd (as happens with good people) was snatched away from us, like Macduff in a different fashion, to become professor of paediatrics in Manchester. Gwyn Williams, from the Mecca of nephrology, Guy's, took over, with the bonus of also being secretary of the Medical Research Society, which gave us some cross fertilisation in our conferences.

Although the senior censor holds that office for only a year, he is already both an experienced examiner and a senior physician; as a full member of the inmost advisory group, he can correct any tendency, should it ever arise, for the college view to be detached from that of the generality of thinking physicians. It is important, I think, that senior censors should be drawn from different places and different branches of the profession. The six senior censors whom I recommended for the office were John Nabarro, Clive Sowry, Malcolm Milne, John Batten, Bill Hoffenberg, and John Dickinson. They were all different, and yet all alike in giving splendid service to the college; and of course it is a particular pleasure that one of them succeeded me as president, before undergoing mutation to Sir Raymond Hoffenberg, KBE, president of Wolfson College, Oxford.

7 A retired life?

Looking back on it, it seems as if I have entered a state of technical retirement by a series of easy stages, each one of them so indefinite that I have been spared the kind of valedictory address which comforts the retirer in some such phrase as, "Now you will have time to do the things which you have always wanted to do." By a combination of good sense and good fortune — mainly the latter — I have almost always managed to make time for doing things that I really wanted to do; and it is no small part of my good fortune that some friendly institution has always been willing to pay me a living wage for doing what I would in any case have wished to do.

I suppose that of the various stages the three most notable were the move from Manchester to the DHSS, which entailed my separation from clinical work; the end of September 1977, when I exchanged my university status of professor (on secondment) for that of professor emeritus; and Monday 28 March 1983 when I handed over the college caduceus (a silver staff presented to the college by John Caius in 1556, and carried by the president on formal occasions). On the first two of these occasions there was a specific new challenge and occupation before my eyes, but on the third the future was indefinite. Fortunately, in a rare burst of foresight, I had realised that when I left the college I would, unless I did something about it, find myself lacking two essentials of continuing activity — an office and a secretary. Still more fortunately, I explained my problem to Peter Williams, director of the Wellcome Trust, and on an informal basis he supplied these two necessities for the next couple of years and more, after which the college expansion enabled me to occupy a room there, as convener of the college committee on ethical aspects of medicine. Without that help I would have been quite unable to produce a pair of small books and undertake some other activities during that period.

I do not know what evidence exists to support the statement so often made that Nature abhors a vacuum; but I do know that I surveyed the prospect of a vacuum of occupation with some apprehension. I need not have worried. By some strange process of quaternary fission I found myself, at different times, president of four organisations. It made an interesting change to have variety in place of executive responsibility. And variety there was, as the organisations were — in chronological order, but with overlapping between them — the Medical Protection Society, the British Medical Association, the Medical Council on Alcoholism, and Health Concern.

Medical practice is a high risk activity, and would still be so even if doctors were infallible — which of course they are not. Patients and their relatives are well capable of perceiving that the outcome either of an operation or of a course of medical treatment is disappointing in the light of their expectations; but it is genuinely difficult for them, or indeed for anyone, to assess whether the outcome was predetermined by the nature of the clinical condition in the first instance, or whether a different course of action might have produced a better result. Although medical treatment may in particular circumstances be just as beneficial or as dangerous as a surgical operation, the finiteness and even the drama of surgery makes it more vulnerable to blame as the cause of a disappointing outcome. It is not even true that the best surgeons always have the best results — for one way of achieving a high rate of success is to operate only on patients who are a good risk and who at the extreme may only doubtfully need the operation. In the past decade or two there has been a greater tendency, not impeded by American lawyers, to look to the doctor or surgeon for compensation for any outcome which has disappointed the patient. Sometimes such claims are fully justified, when there has been a careless mistake that should never have happened; but it is also possible to blame doctors unfairly for a bad outcome which was unavoidable, and it is on this basis that medical defence or protection organisations have grown up.

I am happy to say that until I became its president my own direct involvement with the Medical Protection Society was limited to paying my subscription and reading the cautionary tales in the annual report. But shortly before I was due to leave the Royal College of Physicians my friend John Robertson of Liverpool asked me if I would be interested in becoming president. In due course I was appointed, and I found the meetings of the council and of the cases committee (which considers specific allegations against doctors) very interesting. I found, for example, that the society, like other similar bodies, does not try to defend the indefensible. On the other hand, by providing cover for doctors who are the victims rather than the real authors of misfortunes, it at any rate slows down the harmful advance of over defensiveness in medical practice. For example, if the fear of litigation were such as to force doctors to disclose every possible remote risk in the procedures that they were advising, valuable opportunities of benefit might be lost. That bad cases might make bad law, or at least bad precedent, might have been illustrated by the sad case in which an operation on the spine was followed by the rare and very serious complication of extensive paralysis. The judges in this case took the view that what was required of a surgeon was reasonable care and expertise, and that his duty of communication to the patient did not extend to listing every conceivable risk. Against this it was argued that if the patient had known what was going to happen she would not have had the operation; but it seems to me equally cogent that if the surgeon had known the outcome he would certainly not have done it.

I think that on balance the defence societies have served not only doctors well but also the public, and great credit must be given to our own legal profession for avoiding the transatlantic system of taking up cases of possible medical negligence on what is called a contingency basis — if the action succeeds, the lawyers get a considerable proportion of the damages. As a result, the cost of protection for doctors in the United States has risen to many thousands of dollars a year, a cost which is of course passed on to patients under a free enterprise system. Even in this country the cost of medical insurance, which is obligatory for any holder of an NHS post, is now several hundred pounds a year whereas 10 years ago it was of the order of £25 annually.

It was another friend, John Walton, who first opened with me the question of whether I would care to be considered for the presidency of the British Medical Association, a post which he had himself just held with distinction, as well as the presidency of the General Medical Council. Again, although I had been a member of the BMA for many years, I had not held any office in the association; but I had attended occasional meetings of the BMA council as an observer when I was president of the Royal College of Physicians. I had also come to know the members of the joint consultants committee representing the BMA. Again, as with the Medical Protection Society, the president of the BMA is not expected to exercise the kind of executive function which is carried out by the chairman of council, or by the secretary of the BMA. He gives a formal address at his inauguration — or as formal an address as he is capable of giving; in my own case informality tends to creep in. He also attends meetings of the chief officers of the association in a senior citizen capacity. So far as I can recall, I strayed outside these limits on only one issue but it was the important one of whether investigations could properly be carried out on the fertilised human ovum, before the appearance of the future embryo as the so called primitive streak at around the fourteenth day after conception.

In the medieval church it was commonly held that the male fetus acquired a soul at 40 days after conception, and the female fetus at 80 days. This position was clearly offensive, and not only to feminists; but clerical opinion had rushed to the other extreme, endowing an undifferentiated mass of cells with all the inalienable rights of the Declaration of Independence. Resting as it does on the prior questions, What is life? and What is humanity? the question When does human life begin? suffers from a similar open endedness to the question, How long is a piece of string? Gut feelings and dogma are no substitute for a spirit of inquiry, which can both shed light on the important early stages of development in our own species and enhance the practicality of providing offspring for childless couples — including the practicality of not providing such offspring five or six at a time. As a member of the voluntary licensing authority set up by the MRC and the Royal College of Obstetricians and Gynaecologists to fill what is proving to be a rather long gap between the Warnock report and legislation on these issues, I criticised the term pre-embryo, not only on the grounds that it might be suspected of being a fudge (in the end, this scarcely happened), but also because even pre-embryo exaggerated the extent of determination of what would happen to any particular part of the fertilised ovum during the first two weeks.

During the early months of 1984 these issues were being debated in parliament, and like many others I was concerned lest the BMA, with its very considerable public influence, should give support to a measure which would not of course have brought research in these matters to an end, but might have ensured that this country, in which Edwards and Steptoe had pioneered in vitro fertilisation, would be excluded from future advances. I spoke at council, where it is quite conventional for the president to speak, but also at the annual representative meeting, where his presence is normally formal — though I emphasised that I spoke as a member of council, and not as president. In the event, the annual representative meeting supported by a majority continuing work in this area.

Soon after the end of my one year term as president, Dr John Havard, the secretary of the BMA, asked me to be chairman of the board of science and education. The board has a particular responsibility for the scientific aspects of problems facing the BMA, and this is to some extent analogous to the responsibility of the association's central ethical committee for the ethical aspects of problems. The scientific and the ethical approach to medical problems are complementary to each other, and not inherently or necessarily in conflict; nevertheless there can be differences of emphasis, and it is important that neither of these groupings (board or committee) should have the final voice on an important matter of BMA policy — that is for the council, or even the annual representative meeting. Rather than attempting to give a general account of the way in which the board functions, I will take one specific instance of how a potentially difficult problem has been handled.

Prince Charles was president of the BMA for the year 1981-2, and he asked for a sympathetic examination of methods of healing alternative to conventional medicine. This plea has elicited a response from a number of medical organisations, including the Royal Society of Medicine; but my own involvement with it was in the BMA response. As a member of the working party chaired by Professor James Payne, which was set up by the board of science when Peter Quilliam was chairman, I advised against any attempt to set up a formal controlled trial. There are well over a hundred systems of alternative medicine, and the choice of one or two of them for testing would have been distinctly invidious; more important, it seems inappropriate to apply the methods of scientific appraisal to systems which are proudly unscientific. The working party took a large amount of evidence from representatives of various types of alternative medicine, and produced a somewhat diffuse report which did, however, emphasise the cardinal importance of the best possible definition of the actual problem (that is, the diagnosis) before proceeding to any form of treatment — orthodox, alternative, complementary, or whatever. By the time the report was completed, I had become chairman of the board, and had the responsibility of presenting it to council and to the annual representative meeting. I had persuaded the working party to include a rather astringent summary (on p 76 of the report), which probably assisted the passage of the report through council but did not ensure it a good general press response. I can live with this result, since I believe it may have spared the BMA from a difficult and inconclusive trial of the untestable. More important, the primary responsibility of any doctor is to present and future patients, not to his colleagues, orthodox or otherwise. In a free society, any patient can seek any form of treatment from any healer — always provided that the unqualified healer does not purport to be medically qualified (which is illegal); that he does not charge the patient ruinously; and that he has good evidence that the patient is not suffering from a condition such as appendicitis for which orthodox treatment is critically necessary.

Another presidency which carries no executive responsibility is that of the Medical Council on Alcoholism (MCA), whose governing body is in the capable hands of Sir Reginald Murley, whom I got to know well as president of the Royal College of Surgeons. In the past few years there has been a tendency, both official and unofficial, to demedicalise the problems associated with alcohol, and a number of organisations have sprung up in which the possible medical contribution is discounted. In spite of this, however, the problem has not gone away, and I am among those who believe that doctors have an important part to play. In that light, I welcome the contribution to the education of medical students and doctors made by the MCA. There is an important distinction to be made between the risks associated with smoking and those with the use of alcoholic beverages. Smoking is like radioactivity in this respect, that its harmful effects even at minimal dosage cannot be ruled out — in other words, there is no demonstrable threshold below which exposure can be shown to be safe. On the other hand, a number of studies have indicated that mortality among those who take small amounts of alcohol is actually lower than mortality among total abstainers. This does not, of course, mean that a small intake of alcohol is completely safe, and the consumption of large amounts of alcohol is highly dangerous to health as well as occasioning behaviour more offensive and even dangerous to bystanders than the pollution of air with smoke.

The Medical Protection Society, the BMA, and the Medical Council on Alcoholism have all been in operation for many years, but Health Concern is something new, and so to some extent is the need for it. Although elements of controversy attended the birth of the National Health Service in 1948, it rapidly became accepted by all political parties as a vital component of the welfare state, which again was generally accepted as a good thing. This virtual consensus lasted for a quarter of a century, but the economic recession of the past decade has combined with an increase in the proportion of older people in our population to cause some questioning of the practicality of maintaining the NHS as the major provider of health care. There has been a resurgence of belief that commercial provision of services may be more efficient than provision by the state; the demonology of this belief equates socialists with communists, and administrators with bureaucrats. Although criticism of the NHS has not quite become overt in this country, as it had been in the USA, there has been a distinct thrust towards privatisation, both within the NHS in relation to "hotel services," and also outside the NHS in the encouragement of private organisations for the provision of health care. Although this trend towards privatisation is most consistently opposed by the Labour party and those trade unions with employees in the health service, it is also a source of worry to many outside the Labour party, including many doctors and nurses devoted to the principles of the NHS. About two years ago David Ennals initiated discussions about setting up an organisation aimed at defending the principles of the NHS, and with a membership including professional bodies such as the Royal College of Nursing; trade unions such as the National Union of Public Employees and the Confederation of Health Service Employees; and organisations representing patients. I took part in these discussions, and later agreed to become president of Health Concern, for it is my firm belief that the NHS, imperfect though it may be in particular respects, is by far the best way so far discovered of providing health care. It follows from this that support for it should not be politically polarised, but should embrace all those who hold such a view, irrespective of their political affiliation.

None of these presidencies was or is full time, and I have managed to be concerned in two interesting inquiries, on rather different subjects — the incidence of childhood leukaemia in the neighbourbood of a radioactive plant at Sellafield in Cumbria; and the provision of health care in Guernsey, in the Channel Islands.

In the last century Britain pioneered the industrial revolution based on coal and iron, and later paid the penalty of having obsolete machinery overtaken by newer devices in other countries. Having made a similar early start in developing peaceful applications of nuclear energy, we may now be encountering elements of a similar problem. We have experienced one major fire at Windscale in 1957, and on the combined site of Windscale and Calder Hall, grouped together as Sellafield, there is no doubt some archaic equipment, though a new reprocessing plant is under construction. A team of investigative journalists from Yorkshire Television became interested in the health of workers at Sellafield, and in the course of their inquiry they came across suggestions that children in the village of Seascale were liable to suffer from lymphatic leukaemia. The subsequent programme aroused considerable concern, and I was asked by the CMO, Donald Acheson, if I would get together a group to make an independent investigation into the problem.

As the assessment of the incidence of leukaemia is primarily an epidemiological problem, three of the six colleagues whom I asked to serve were epidemiologists of distinction — Abe Adelstein, Martin Gardner and Geoffrey Rose. The other three were a physicist (Stewart Orr), a radiobiologist (Roger Berry), and a clinical geneticist (Martin Bobrow). We were hedged in on all sides by special interests — the nuclear power industry, the fossil fuel industries, environmental pressure groups, and a selection of government departments — not all with health at the core of their interests. Some of our witnesses raised the impossible demand for absolute safety, while at the other extreme there were dire predictions of economic ruin if the nuclear industry were trammelled in any way. I think we managed to preserve independence, and on only one occasion did I have to advise a civil servant from a department (other than the DHSS) to look up the meaning of independent in a good dictionary.

The report that we produced gives the details of our inquiry, but in essence it boiled down to trying to get answers to three questions. First, Was there an excess of environmental radioactivity near Sellafield? Given the amounts of radioactive material being dealt with on the site, the qualitative answer to this question must be Yes; but the measurements on which a precise quantitative answer could be based were quite hard to come by, and one of our recommendations was that monitoring should be more frequently carried out. But even on the worst case estimate, the excess radioactivity from the plant would be a small proportion of natural background radiation from cosmic rays and terrestrial radioactive minerals.

The second question, Was there an excess of childhood leukaemia in the area? is more difficult to answer with precision, because of the uncertainty inherent in surveys which start off based on index cases, rather than on a previously defined population over a given period of time. There was, however, a considerable probability that the incidence of lymphatic leukaemia in childhood near Sellafield over a 30 year period was higher than expected; but the actual number of cases was small, making even a probable estimate imprecise.

The third question is quite difficult to phrase and impossible to answer, but it is the key to the whole thing so an attempt must be made. If the answer to questions one and two is a somewhat shaded Yes, is the excess of radioactivity the cause of the excess of childhood leukaemia? Anyone who has tried to demonstrate causality in other contexts, including such clear cut cases as smoking and lung cancer, will realise the difficulty. Others were less conscious of it, and confidently predicted a causal relationship.

On the information available to us we felt able to offer a qualified reassurance to residents in the neighbourhood, and people actually living there were on the whole grateful for what they judged to be an honest appraisal of the evidence. But environmental groups were far from satisfied, and in the interval since the report appeared they have seized on disclosures that some emissions from Sellafield were not reported to our group; and the controversy has of course been rekindled by the Chernobyl disaster, in spite of the obvious differences between that and anything that has ever happened at Sellafield. While the actual risk of Sellafield has not been increased by these more recent happenings, the perceived risk must have been so, and the future of nuclear power has re-entered political debate, if indeed it ever left it. No source of the amount of energy required by an industrial nation can possibly be free from risks; and coal and oil each bring their casualties and fatalities to the work force. Perhaps the ratio of perceived to actual risk is higher for nuclear energy because of the hidden nature of the hazard, and the unquantified risk of long term genetic damage. Another of our recommendations was for a continuing organisation to keep health aspects of nuclear energy under review; and this has not only been accepted, it has been acted upon with the establishment of the DHSS committee on medical aspects of radiation in the environment (COMARE), chaired by Martin Bobrow.

A rather different, and in some ways more pleasant, assignment was a survey of the provision of health care in Guernsey. As independent fiefs of the crown, the Channel Islands do not participate directly in the NHS, although for specified purposes they use NHS facilities on the mainland. Both in Guernsey and in Jersey primary medical care is provided by general practitioners in the private sector, but the arrangements for specialist services are different. In Jersey, hospital services are provided mainly by specialists provided by the States of Jersey; whereas in Guernsey, specialist services are provided by members of the independent general practices who have acquired the necessary specialised experience during training. As there are six group practices on the island there are also six surgeons, which seems a little luxurious for a resident population of 55 000. The hospital in St Peter Port is provided by the States of

Guernsey, and inpatient treatment is free, whereas outpatient treatment has to be paid for by the patient. There are about 48 doctors on the island, each of whom in rotation provides night cover for emergencies in the hospital. On the mainland in the NHS, where junior doctors are struggling to change from one in two rotas to one in three, the thought of a one in 48 rota may stimulate envy, but it can scarcely cultivate finely honed expertise in emergency care. I have mentioned these slight bizarreries in the system not to denigrate it but to make the point that apparently illogical systems can still work rather well; for in fact the doctors are generally satisfied with the system, and the patients are reasonably content except when prolonged illness leads to high cost.

I was again fortunate in the colleagues who agreed to help me in the survey, notably Dr W J E McKee, regional medical officer for Wessex, who in addition to his own expertise in the provision of health care provided the secretarial backing from his own staff; and also Dr Howard Baderman (emergency medicine), Dr Nigel Compston (general medicine), Mr Pharic Gillibrand (obstetrics), Dr Denis Pereira Gray (general practice), Dr P N Nott (psychiatry), Mr John Webster (surgery) and Dr D J Pearce (anaesthesia).

We spent five days on the island, and made a number of suggestions, mainly in the direction of strengthening the hospital services by a greater provision of full time specialists. The system of private general practice seems well established, and we did not think it wise to upset it on doctrinaire grounds. Our report was primarily to the States of Guernsey, and not directly to our medical colleagues on the island, but I believe we were sufficiently tender to a system which perhaps conformed more to the real needs of the island than to theories of health service provision.

At about the time I left the Royal College of Physicians I was invited by Gordon McLachlan to give a Rock Carling lecture, the suggested subject being the division of medical care between the hospital and the community. I did not warm greatly to the theme as I felt it was somewhat limited, and I was also rather out of sympathy with the conventional wisdom that many of the problems of long term care of physical and mental illness can be solved by transfer out of hospital. This may be true if resources are transferred along with patients, and more true if resources are actually increased, for it must be more expensive to provide the same facilities in a larger number of places. But what seemed to me the major insight, as I thought about the problem, was that at least some formulations of it exaggerated the division between hospital and community as if they were separate worlds, whereas the hospital is actually part of the community and they should be working in collaboration. This example of what I regarded as a false antithesis led me on to think of others, and I eventually built up the requisite monograph and lecture on the more general theme, describing the ultimate collection or concoction as *An Anthology of False Antitheses*. By way of illustration, in addition to the original antithesis between hospital and community, I added what I regarded as false antitheses between pure and applied science; the science and the art of medicine; the medicine of individuals and of populations; curing and caring; treatment and prevention; and for good measure a few others.

Soon after completing the Rock Carling monograph I was given another writing opportunity, in the shape of a request to contribute a book on medicine to the series *Invitation to . . .* published by Blackwell. The idea was to give sixth formers contemplating going into medicine some general idea of what they might be letting themselves in for; but I felt that a simple outline of the scope of clinical medicine might also be of interest to lay people in general, and perhaps more particularly to biologists, physicists, or chemists who have become members of teams working with patients. I wrote the book in three main sections, giving a general indication, first, of the kinds of knowledge relevant to medical practice; second, of the application of medical knowledge and techniques — including the important techniques of history taking and examination — to the individual patient; and third, of the application of medical and epidemiological expertise to improving the public health.

When cudgelling my brains to dream up some recreations to enter into *Who's Who*, I hit on reading and writing, for it would have been ostentatious, even if truthful, to say "most work." Both the items which I chose are true — I am uneasy if I have nothing to read, and I really enjoy writing once I have made a start. But they are not fully comprehensive. I also enjoy music, though I fear that on that well known desert island all my discs would be preternaturally square — baroque music above all, with Bach at the summit. Also I enjoy travel, and am happy that it has not ceased with retirement; but we each of us enjoy our own travelogues better than anyone else's, and I shall be merciful. Looking at pictures has been another great joy of my life, and I usually manage to exchange at least one session of any conference abroad for a visit to a gallery that I have not seen before and am unlikely to see again.

Such have been the refreshments of my life. In my final chapter I shall, greatly daring, parade my speculations on what it has all been about — after all, I am Scotch, even if I have spent two thirds of my life "abroad."

8 Questions without answers

In choosing a title for this chapter I have compromised between an indicative one (which I suppose might be "Politics, ethics, and religion") and an evocative title such as "Songs without words" (which gives nothing away and is relevant only to the emotional appeal, but also the ineffability, of some of the matters to be discussed).

Politics I regard as a means to an end, the end being the health and welfare of individuals rather than the aggrandisement of the state, still less of politicians themselves. But even if I cannot in any way fully satisfy it, because of other interests and preoccupations, I am mindful of the claim of Pericles on behalf of the citizens of Athens: "Our citizens attend both to public and private duties, and do not allow absorption in their own various affairs to interfere with their knowledge of the city's."

My formal participation in politics, however, has been limited to casting my vote. At one time I had two of these, one as a St Andrews graduate and one as a general citizen; but the first of them has been swept away in our determined pursuit of what I call inverted élitism, by which I mean the grinding down of any privilege which might be construed as leading to meritocracy — the idea of a revolution based on the university vote being somewhat far fetched. At present my vote is somewhat nugatory, as it is cast in Michael Heseltine's constituency of South Oxfordshire. It has also changed over time, so I expect I qualify as a floating voter. Although I have never voted for communism, the "greens," or Screaming Lord Sutch, I have at different times voted Conservative, Labour, Liberal, and SDP, more or less in that order. The SDP have now come out with a health policy that faithfully recapitulates the mistakes made by Barbara Castle in extruding private health care from the NHS, in the interests of pseudoequality, so I shall probably try something else.

Although some of my professional inquiries such as the one on Sellafield have had political implications, the only political cause which I have persistently held to is that which should concern us all, the preservation of peace. To begin with two naive assumptions, I believe that every person of sanity and good will desires peace; and that he should desire it for other people as well as for himself. The naivety of these assumptions is starkly revealed by a glance at our war torn world, with countries like Iraq and Iran at one another's throats for a period longer than the second world war. There must be many people who intellectually would give assent to my two naive propositions but nevertheless act in direct opposition to them, either because their employment depends on the manufacture or use of arms, or more wickedly because they are actually engaged in illicit arms supply. I suppose the word illicit implies that some manufacture or use of arms is licit — something which I see as a dangerous anachronism left over from the medieval concept of a just war. This concept includes two requirements: that the cause for which the war is fought must itself be just; and that the war is one which could be won. The first of these concepts was used to justify the crusades against the Mohammedans, and is occasionally dusted off to validate the creation of bulwarks against communism. The second concept is the more anachronistic of the two, for it seems to be fairly generally agreed that in a nuclear war both sides would be losers.

Both sides in the current arms race speak, without conscious hypocrisy, of defence, and on our side of the unwinnable conflict we speak of deterrence. The grandiloquent phrase, "the philosophy of deterrence," may be of recent coinage, but its roots go far back into history. In the days of Macaulay, no doubt every schoolboy knew the meaning of Si vis pacem, para bellum; the sinister translation of it is, "If you want peace, prepare for war." Now that may have been all very well for the Romans, once the Roman peace had been established, and only disorganised primitive tribes were to be reckoned with (when it came to the Parthians or the Alemanni, things did not work out so well). And when we have a confrontation between two massive powers or groups, each armed with nuclear weapons, the validity of the concept of deterrence could be tested only by an experiment that cannot be performed. I cannot deny the proposition, often made, that the so called peace which we have enjoyed since 1945 is due to our nuclear shield; but neither do I entirely accept it: it seems to me just as possible that even power drunk leaders may shrink from starting a nuclear war, now that deterrence is as it were, two way. So we have a dangerous mixture of fear and aggression.

Am I about to reveal myself as that dangerous warmonger, a unilateralist? I am not, and for a quite particular reason, which entails a short digression into recent history. Our stand against the Nazi hegemony, for some time alone in the world as belligerents — and that perhaps *was* the last just war — gave us, I believe, a certain amount of moral capital even in a world of realpolitik. And at that time a unilateral abjuration of nuclear weapons by Britain might have had some effect. But in 1956 the tragic combination of a sick Prime Minister trapped in his memories of Munich, a cynical French regime, and — with most excuse — a beleaguered state of Israel, brought about our botched invasion of Suez. I was in Baltimore at the time, and saw at first hand the anger and disappointment of many Americans; and the Russians took advantage of the occasion to invade a Hungary struggling to be free of them. We suffered a moral slump, and also demonstrated our relative weakness. More recently, the Falklands affair — into which we were admittedly forced — has shown that we still have some strength, but it has not done much to restore the moral standing which we lost; and it also showed what a vicious thing even conventional war is, waged with modern weaponry.

Rightly or wrongly, I believe that our unilateral renunciation of nuclear arms would now be an empty gesture. Instead, we should be pressing for first of all a standstill, and then a reduction of both nuclear and conventional weapons. What we should not be doing is yapping encouragement at one of the great powers to go further and further along the road of mutually assured destruction. Science fiction terms like "star wars" do not promote the cause of peace. My trust in summits falls some way short of blind faith, but I welcome them in the hope that some actual human contact may serve to loosen in some small degree the chains forged by the armament makers, strategic modellers, and similar hawks on both sides.

In holding these views, I do not think I am anti-patriotic, anti-American, pro-Russian, or hostile to law and order. But I would rather be accused of one or all of these things than refrain from drawing attention to the greatest visible threat before us. A doctor has a duty to point to specific dangers which come within his own expertise; but it is as a citizen that I add my small voice to the appeal for survival.

Although I have for many years been interested both in the practical content and in the theoretical basis of medical ethics, my attention has been more sharply and immediately focused by the need from time to time to give lectures and addresses on various themes with a manifest ethical component. For example, I acquired the responsibility of giving a general talk on medical ethics to the students of Manchester University; I gave the Desmond Curran lecture at St George's Hospital on an ethical theme; and I am the convener of the committee on ethical aspects of medicine at the Royal College of Physicians.

My responsibility for lecturing to the Manchester students was to some extent thrust upon me; but at least it was thrust upon me, with some hesitation, by my own hand. It came about in this way. When I succeeded Robert Platt in the Manchester chair, it seemed a suitable moment to review all the lectures for which the department of medicine was responsible. In addition to those given by the staff of the medical unit, many of the lectures in clinical medicine were given by colleagues in cardiology, neurology, and so on;

but in addition there were lectures on medical history and medical ethics, for which the professor of medicine also held ultimate responsibility. I found that the students were having three lectures in medical ethics, all of them given by a general practitioner, and largely concerned with what would now be called practice management and with those rules of minimum decent conduct which would avoid any close encounter with the law or the General Medical Council. I was not too happy with this, for it seemed to me that many of the important problems of medical ethics arose in hospital practice; and also I felt that too much emphasis was being placed on the minimum standard of staying within the established rules. The family doctor concerned had an attitude to lectures which was happily less than proprietorial, so I was able to reduce his share of them from three to one, which gave room for a lecture on other aspects. I asked Robert Platt to do this, but found later that his lecture had been confined to problems related to normal and deviant sex. Important as these are, they are certainly not the whole story, and I persuaded Robert in time to let this (then) young man have a go.

In my reckoning, ethical medical practice requires both moral and scientific probity. The most unethical thing that a practising doctor can do is to let his competence fall away; in other aspects of his practice he will sooner or later be pulled up by the law or by the judgment of his peers, but his ability to practise competently is primarily a burden on his own conscience. Similarly, I take the view that ethics committees in judging research projects should take the scientific aspects of the proposal into account, calling in additional expertise to do so if necessary. Not only unethical procedures, but also scientifically unsound research can have bad consequences.

Although I have no particular competence to consider the philosophical basis of medical ethics, it is tempting to say something of the matter, while acknowledging that I have neither the breadth nor the depth of someone like Raanan Gillon, whose series of articles in the *British Medical Journal* in 1985 must have increased the interest and understanding of many doctors. There appear to be two main orientations in this matter, one which deduces ethical conduct from primary ethical principles (deontological), and one which works back to ethical judgments from consideration of their consequences (utilitarian). The term deontological may suggest a theistic basis for ethical principles, but this is not a necessary component of the deontological view, even though I personally find it easier to understand than seeing ethical principles as a byproduct of evolution by "witless Nature."

The great weakness of the deontological orientation is the obvious flagrant disagreement in the ethical stances of different individuals. As a pragmatist, I find utilitarianism more immediately appealing; but it has the great danger that it can fairly easily, by concentrating on the end, create indifference to the validity of the means; and the history of this century is one sad long object lesson that the end does not justify the means. Carrying my pragmatism further, I am led to a belief in "situation ethics," which has elements both of deontology and of utilitarianism, the one tempering the other. The deontological element in my own belief is my feeling that we are ultimately dependent on our own good conscience, however that is derived; but a utilitarian element is equally necessary, to protect us from the fanaticism that may make us inflict on other people our own ethical framework, which they may not share. I am exceedingly suspicious of apparently absolute rules and formulations; it is so easy to misapply them to a situation which they do not fit, they are often in conflict with one another, and the variety of actual particulate decisions is such that even Procrustes could not devise a universal frame. I am not, of course, claiming that it is hard to lay down ethical rules — too many people have done so to make that proposition tenable. But the real dilemma is twofold, and it may be appropriate to phrase it in the form of two questions: first, When two well founded principles conflict, which is to prevail? and second, A principle having been stated, how does one legitimise exceptions?

Let me try to illuminate, and perhaps lighten, that sketchy

theoretical discussion by saying something of the particular problem which has been largely responsible for making me think along these lines. Mounting concern that information held about individuals might be used to their disadvantage, they themselves being ignorant of the matter, led to the introduction of the Data Protection Bill, which in due course became an act (1985). Unusually perhaps, the title of the bill gave a clear definition of its purpose; but it was obvious that there might be special problems related to information held about individuals by doctors and other health professionals. On the one hand, disclosure might be necessary in the public interest — for example, to control the spread of infection, or to prevent terrorism or other forms of murder. On the other hand, the right of individuals to have access to information held about them, including the right to check its accuracy, might likewise not be absolute, as the information divulged to them might on occasion be hurtful to their peace of mind, or even their physical health. I became chairman of an interprofessional working group to consider these matters; we have met on over 50 occasions, spread over a couple of years (shades of *Inequalities in Health*), and I have to admit that some aspects remain unresolved. The problem cannot be described as untouched, but it still awaits complete resolution; for although the act has become law, the regulations governing its implementation are still on rather weather beaten stocks. It would be cruel to burden you with our deliberations at any length; but let me use facets of the problem to flesh out the two questions stated above.

WHEN TWO WELL FOUNDED PRINCIPLES CONFLICT, WHICH IS TO PREVAIL?

Most people would agree that information on an individual's health should not be divulged without his consent, and also that access to medical information by reputable epidemiologists is important, which gives it ethical value. If absolute priority is given to the first of these considerations, much valuable epidemiological research, such as that which showed the association between smoking and lung cancer, would be prevented from taking place. If absolute priority is given to the second consideration, it would allow, for example, the publication of lists of names to confer additional validity on epidemiological papers, and allow subsequent investigators to review the original data completely. Almost all of my group were willing to allow access by qualified epidemiologists to the records of patients who for one or another reason were unable to give consent, provided that the names of individuals did not appear in any publication. A certain degree of justification for this view may be seen in the concept of implied consent — that is, an individual who has voluntarily sought treatment, and thus initiated a medical record, may be considered to approve of its use in reputable research. But one or two of us would have none of this, even though I pointed out, in my pragmatic way, the difficulty of obtaining informed consent from the comatose, the mad, and even the dead.

A PRINCIPLE HAVING BEEN STATED, HOW DOES ONE LEGITIMISE EXCEPTIONS?

The principle of non-disclosure of records is clear, categorical, and enshrined in the Data Protection Act. But what about exceptions? Early versions of the bill included exceptions for the detection of tax evasion or illegal immigration. But the range of permitted exceptions has come down to matters such as prevention of terrorism (with which almost everyone would agree), or the prevention or detection of serious crime (on which there is less agreement, and also a need to define serious crime, though fortunately there is a reasonable definition of this in the Police and Criminal Evidence Bill, which was going through parliament at about the same time). In a Granada Television programme some years ago the barrister Paul Sieghart (who later became a most valuable member of the interprofessional working group) raised the hypothetical case of a woman who came to her doctor, confessing that she had agreed to smuggle in some diamonds by swallowing a small bag containing them, and unfortunately it had failed to appear. Should the doctor tell the police? Most people thought not, and then, as the rules of the game allowed, Paul revised the scenario converting the diamonds into a cache of heroin and also adding that a gang were concerned who might kill the woman if the truth became known. This additional information divided the group, and I for one fell halfway between the diamonds and the heroin. What I hope I may have indicated in an oblique way is that general exceptions are difficult to sustain — so much depends on the particular case, including the individuals concerned therein.

I would like to add a final touch of originality to these unconventional memoirs by saying something of religion. In this century the permissive society has rather tediously swept away our inhibitions on discussing sex, including its bizarre deviations; and from opposite ends of the spectrum of opinion, the euthanasia society and the hospice movement have removed the taboo on discussion of death. But as Rose Macaulay pointed out, in *The Towers of Trebizond*, personal religion — so freely talked about in previous centuries — is now an embarrassment in conversation: "It is a most strange thing that this important part of human life, the struggle that almost everyone has about good and evil, cannot now be talked of without embarrassment, unless of course one is in church . . . you cannot say to your friends that you would like to be good, they would think you were going Buchmanite, or Grahamite, or something else that you would not at all care to be thought."

Like another doctor before me, though without his grace of style and character, I can follow Sir Thomas Browne in daring "without usurpation" to "assume the honourable Stile of a Christian." This is perhaps to be more faithful to my upbringing than to the general drift of my matured profession — even in their own times Dr Montaigne's virtual silence on religion in his *Essais* was more typical than

Browne's discourse on it, in which he gives "the general scandal of my Profession" as one of the reasons to suggest that he might be without religion; and since then the opening up of large tracts of medicine to a scientific approach has perhaps made it easier for doctors to limit themselves to that way of thinking. In other fields of thought, the ideas of a heaven above and a hell beneath have somewhat lost currency; if spoken about at all, they are allegorised away.

Responses to this altered view of the world have been various. Now, as in past ages, the generality of people, whatever their professions of belief, are probably in their hearts like Gallio of Achaia, who "cared for none of these things," and just get on with the business of living. The primrose path down which Pangloss led Candide, of believing that everything was for the best in the best of all possible worlds, leads by another route to the more or less contented cultivation of one's own garden, cynically or hedonistically as the case may be. But for those who recognise or imagine that there are matters beyond the treadmill of daily life, and matters on which the reasoned scientific approach has little or no bearing, two main reactions have developed, which seem to me to lie at the root of the current conflicts or discussions within the Anglican communion.

The traditionalist approach, currently exercised in deprecating the ordination of women and the speculations of the Bishop of Durham, relies on a deposit of faith, encapsulated in the ancient creeds, and guarded by bishops in a succession from the twelve apostles. What is actually believed and taught changes from time to time, but this process of development, to use Newman's term, is under the charge of a church whose individual members and even leaders are fallible, but in which the teaching *ex cathedra* is not subject to error. Within such a system there is plenty of scope for dispute on the nature of the church, on the degrees and circumstances of infallibility, and on the legitimacy of the ultramontanism and triumphalism, even at times theatricality, which may encumber an extreme Catholic position. But the essence of the matter is a willing submission to authority.

By contrast, the liberal approach appears to play down submission to authority, and to uphold the ultimate primacy of private judgment, which was established for those who adhere to the Reformation. The Reformation has had some strange fruits, in a multiplicity of incongruous sects; and those with a strong appetite for authoritative guidance tend to favour the more dogmatic expression of the traditionalist approach.

It would not be for an ignorant doctor to assess which, if either, of these approaches is closer to the truth. My own upbringing and my devotion to science and especially medicine, which deals almost always with probabilities and not with certainties, make me lean to the liberal approach. This is not a matter open to experiment, and we have to turn instead to faith, hope, and charity. My personal confession is that my faith is uncertain, my hope variable, but my love for what I know of Jesus from the gospels is strong. My sins, though real, have perhaps been of a different kind from those so freely confessed by James Boswell, but perhaps I can end by saying with him, "My great object is to attain a proper conduct in life. How sad will it be if I turn out no better than I am."